Researching Social Media with Children

Reflecting on the methodological issues involved in researching digital spaces with children, this book shares good practices and delves into the ethics of such research.

Social media has completely redefined how children and young people relate to each other, express themselves, and present their identities and sexualities. Yet researching social media can be a difficult and daunting task given the ephemerality of the content, its contextual hyperspecificity, the complex power relationships between users, celebrity culture, digital capitalism, and the ethical issues that arise from the reimagining of the public/private space. Using digital ethnography and creative digital storytelling workshops with children and young people aged 13–15 and 13–18 on TikTok, Instagram, and Twitch, this book studies their interactions, language, codes, the risks they take, and the victimizations they suffer.

Researching Social Media with Children will be of use to social scientists conducting online research, and to students and scholars of media studies, digital criminology, psychology, and sociology.

[The authors draw on experiences from studies carried out in Spain on children and social media by the Knowledge-Research Group on Social Problems at Universidad Europea de Madrid.]

Antonio Silva Esquinas holds a bachelor's in criminology, extraordinary award (Universitat Oberta de Catalunya), master's in social and cultural anthropology (Universidad Nacional de Educación a Distancia), and doctorate in anthropology and criminology (Universidad Nacional de Educación a Distancia). He is a lecturer of criminology (Universidad Europea de Madrid), main methodologist, and ethnographer at Grupo Conocimiento-Investigación en Problemáticas Sociales.

Jorge Ramiro Pérez Suárez holds a bachelor's in law from Universidad Complutense de Madrid, a master's in criminology and criminal justice from the University of Edinburgh, and a doctorate in criminology from the University of Huddersfield. He is a senior lecturer in criminology applied to digital spaces at Universidad Europea de Madrid and a researcher at Grupo Conocimiento-Investigación en Problemáticas Sociales.

Raquel Rebeca Cordero Verdugo holds a bachelor's in political science and sociology from Universidad Nacional de Educación a Distancia, postgraduate degree in politics and government (Universidad Nacional de Educación a Distancia), and a doctorate in communication from the perspective of conflict (Universidad Europea de Madrid). She is a senior lecturer in applied sociology and a principal researcher at Grupo Conocimiento-Investigación en Problemáticas Sociales.

Julio Díaz Galán holds a bachelor's in philosophy from Universidad Complutense de Madrid and a doctorate in philosophy (Universidad Nacional de Educación a Distancia). He is a senior lecturer in philosophical anthropology at Universidad Europea de Madrid and a researcher at Grupo Conocimiento-Investigación en Problemáticas Sociales.

Researching Social Media with Children

with Children

#DigitalEthnography #Storytelling

Antonio Silva Esquinas,
Jorge Ramiro Pérez Suárez,
Raquel Rebeca Cordero Verdugo and
Julio Díaz Galán

Routledge
Taylor & Francis Group

LONDON AND NEW YORK

Designed cover image: gettyimages.com

First published 2025

by Routledge

4 Park Square, Milton Park, Abingdon, Oxon OX14 4RN

and by Routledge

605 Third Avenue, New York, NY 10158

Routledge is an imprint of the Taylor & Francis Group, an informa business

British Library Cataloguing in Publication Data
A catalogue record for this book is available from the British Library

Library of Congress Cataloging-in-Publication Data
Names: Silva Esquinas, Antonio, author. | Pérez Suárez, Jorge Ramiro,
author. | Cordero Verdugo, Rebeca, author. | Galán, Julio Díaz, author.
Title: Researching social media with children : #digitalethnography
#storytelling / Antonio Silva Esquinas, Jorge Ramiro Pérez Suárez, Raquel
Rebeca Cordero Verdugo and Julio Díaz Galán.
Description: Abingdon, Oxon ; New York, NY : Routledge, [2025] |
Includes bibliographical references and index.
Identifiers: LCCN 2024015592 (print) | LCCN 2024015593 (ebook) | ISBN
9781032502915 (hardback) | ISBN 9781032506173 (paperback) | ISBN
9781003399315 (ebook)
Subjects: LCSH: Internet and children. | Social media. | Social media and
teenagers. | Digital ethnology.
Classification: LCC HQ784.I58 S57 2025 (print) | LCC HQ784.I58 (ebook) |
DDC 302.23/1083–dc23/eng/20240412
LC record available at https://lccn.loc.gov/2024015592
LC ebook record available at https://lccn.loc.gov/2024015593

ISBN: 978-1-032-50291-5 (hbk)
ISBN: 978-1-032-50617-3 (pbk)
ISBN: 978-1-003-39931-5 (ebk)
DOI: 10.4324/9781003399315

Typeset in Sabon
by Taylor & Francis Books

Contents

Illustrations

Acknowledgements

We would like to acknowledge the help of the European University of Madrid (UEM) and its School of Social Sciences and Communication, its dean, Francisco García Pascual, as well as its Department of Legal Sciences and Humanities. Also, the help received from the Vice-Rectorate of Faculty and Research, the School of Doctorate and Research (EDI), the Office for the Transfer of Research Results (OTRI), Banco Santander, and the Union of Family Associations (UNAF).

We want to thank all the families, young people, and professionals who took part in our studies and workshops, for being so kind and accessible and for sharing their innermost thoughts, knowledge, hopes, and worries. We are profoundly grateful. Thank you for believing in us and in our projects and to want to build a safer and better world.

List of abbreviations

Abbreviation	Spanish / English
5G (EN/SP)	quinta generación / fifth generation
AAA (EN)	Asociación Antropológica Americana / American Anthropological Association
AI (EN)	inteligencia artificial / artificial intelligence
AoIR (EN)	Asociación de Investigadores de Internet / Association of Internet Researchers
ASA (EN)	Asociación Sociológica Americana / American Sociological Association
CBR (EN)	investigación basada en retos / challenge-based research
CIPI (SP)	Comité Investigador Proyecto Interno / Research Committee Internal Project
COVID (EN)	enfermedad del coronavirus / coronavirus disease
CRUE (SP)	Conferencia de Rectores de las Universidades Españolas / Spanish University Rectors' Conference
CSIC (SP)	Consejo Superior de Investigaciones Científicas / High Council for Scientific Research
DIN (GER)	Instituto Alemán de Normalización / German Institute for Standardization
DJ (EN)	disc jockey / disc jockey
EHEA (EN)	Espacio Europeo de Educación Superior / European Higher Education Area
GCIPS (SP)	Grupo Conocimiento-Investigación en Problemáticas Sociales / Knowledge-Research Group on Social Problems

GIF (EN)	formato de intercambio de gráficos / graphics interchange format
INE (SP)	Instituto Nacional de Estadística / National Statistics Institute
IRE (EN)	ética de investigación en internet / internet research ethics
MARVEL (SP)	Multivariable Analítico para la Reflexión Ética Longitudinal / Multivariate Analysis for Reflecting and Validating Ethics Longitudinally
OTRI (SP)	Oficina de Transferencia de Resultados de Investigación / Office for the Transfer of Research Results
POV (EN)	punto de vista / point of view
RRSS (SP)	redes sociales / social media
SDG (EN)	objetivos de desarrollo sostenible / sustainable development goals
UEM (SP)	Universidad Europea de Madrid / European University of Madrid
UNAF (SP)	Unión de Asociaciones Familiares / Union of Family Associations
UNESCO (EN)	Organización de las Naciones Unidas para la Educación, la Ciencia, y la Cultura / United Nations Educational, Scientific, and Cultural Organization

1 Logging in

An introduction

1.1. Who are we (excellent question)?

The Grupo de Conocimiento e Investigación en Problemáticas Sociales, or Knowledge and Research Group on Social Problems (GCIPS), belonging to the Faculty of Social Sciences and Communication of Universidad Europea de Madrid, was launched in 2017. Since then, it went through a number of phases before becoming consolidated in 2020. At that time, the group began to have international repercussions, which is evident from the number of invitations it has received to take part in conferences, seminars, and roundtables.

Characterised by the cross-disciplinary nature of its researchers, offering a combination of criminology, sociology, law, philosophy, and anthropology, its work has focused on three lines of research: 1) phenomenology and social epistemology, 2) technology, crime, and victimisation, and 3) inequality, social exclusion, and public health.

1.2. What have we done?

We have presented two projects here. On the one hand, there is Project A.I.Driana: Development of a Preventive Tool through Storytelling, as part of a digital ethnography on practices and experiences related to youth vulnerability in digital settings (2021/ UEM26[1] – CIPI 21300 6.48[2]). On the other hand, there is Social Media and Antinormative Behaviour in Young People between the ages of 13 and 18. Detecting New Forms of Domination, Addiction and Relationships in the Digital Society. CONFIDOMINA2.NET

DOI: 10.4324/9781003399315-1

(2022/UEM22[3] – CIPI 22–260[4]). These two projects focus on the youth population, digital settings, toxic relationships, and vulnerability and reflect on all three lines of research mentioned above, given the very nature of the phenomenon studied here.

The "digital life" of young people and their ways of behaving and relating have become a global phenomenon that cannot be dismissed. Therefore, studies like the ones proposed here are essential for understanding and taking action in this reality. The changes that the digital world has brought about in social values and models must be reviewed, analysed, and studied in depth to determine the possible consequences they have for society and for individuals.

The normalisation of social media in everyday life has led young people to face a reality that they seem to believe they understand and control, but the volume and complexity of it render it unmanageable. This increases the degree of victimisation of minors. However, it is impossible to expect youths to stop exposing themselves to the digital world. Social media is part of their socialisation environment, their shared habitat. Therefore, aiming for a complete lack of a digital footprint as a means of prevention would be quixotic. Digital educational communities are the first ones to make this impossible by demanding that their students be registered in them. Schools, which are in charge of managing them, forget the impact that such communities may have on the lives of students who are bullied, for example. Thus, schools may unwittingly be opening up a channel for victimisers to enter the victims' most private sphere, their homes, by means of cyberbullying. The minor's home then ceases to be a safe space, compounding their suffering.

Furthermore, the penetration of digital identity into the intimate realm of the collective individual has also led to a breakdown of the boundary between the technological and the biological, as ventured by the author of the *Cyborg Manifesto* (Haraway, 1990). We feel that the study of the social situation must be approached from the perspective of this new reality.

In addition, the precarious mental health of youths resulting from their risky online behaviour (Observatorio Nacional de Tecnología y Sociedad, 2022), the new forms of crime they face, and the diverse expressions of direct or indirect violence affecting them pose a risk today, as evidenced by the increase in the number of suicides (Khatcherian, 2022), that must be remedied.

1.3. What approaches and methods have we used?

In an effort to help solve the problem, from an epistemological viewpoint our research is based on ultra-realism (Hall & Winlow, 2020) and the diverse approaches of *zemiology*, or the theory of social harm (Raymen, 2020). These analytical perspectives are necessary in order to address complex and all-encompassing phenomena like the digital world. The projects mentioned above are intended to have a positive impact on society, generating social transformation and change.

In terms of methodology, the mixed methodologies of Spanish ultra-realism (Silva & Pérez, 2020; Silva, 2024), which consider that qualitative and quantitative methodologies must be integrated to afford a holistic view of the phenomenon being studied, have been applied. The English-speaking school also seems to be gradually moving toward this strategy.

As a research group, we saw the need to launch a series of research projects on minors and social media. This was based on the fact that in one of our previous research projects, focusing on the adult population,[5] we found that minors used these kinds of applications and interacted with adults.

In late 2020, we began the first phase of Project CON-FIDOMINA2.NET, which was implemented parallel with Project A.I.DRIANA. Both projects are geared toward gaining an experiential understanding of the relationship that young people have with the digital world.

A sequential exploratory model was used for the research design, set up from a perspective of transformative social justice (Creswell, 2015). However, for operational purposes, it was deemed necessary to establish a certain degree of simultaneity in executing the phases to make it easier to conduct an adequate integrative analysis of the data attained, thus ensuring the lowest possible number of contradictions in terms of epistemology and sampling (Cordero et al., 2021).

For CONFIDOMINA2.NET, we created two focus groups with fathers, mothers, and professionals in academic orientation and psychology. Along with this, a multi-sited digital ethnography was conducted on TikTok, Twitch, and Instagram, where 15 youth profiles of various genders and more than 10,000 videos were analysed. Finally, an online survey was carried out at public, private, and charter schools in several cities in Spain.

For A.I.DRIANA, we worked with a digital ethnography that entailed the creation of a storytelling workshop (Lambert & Hessler, 2018) on private Instagram and TikTok accounts with seven boys and girls total. In addition, several rounds of interviews were held with their parents (before and after the workshops), and the Delphi method (García-Ruiz & Lena-Acebo, 2018) was applied with a sample composed of professionals in the fields of psychology, sexology, education, and intervention and a digital content creator.

Ethical considerations were taken into account at all times in the implementation of the studies. Our research group is strongly committed to research ethics and follows the criteria set out by the Association of Internet Researchers (Franzke et al., 2020) at all times, using the MARVEL (Multivariate Analysis for Reflecting and Validating Ethics Longitudinally) protocol as a guide to responsible, reflexive research in terms of design, fieldwork, analysis, and dissemination (Silva, 2024).

Furthermore, the fact that we were working with minors led us to be highly scrupulous when developing tools and regarding data protection. This matter was taken into account in the survey design in which the minimum age for answering the survey was set at 14, one year more than the minimum age of the population being studied. Pursuant to Organic Law 3/2018, of 5 December, on the Protection of Personal Data and Safeguarding of Digital Rights, minors' rights are subject to special protection in Spain. Indeed, Article 7 of this law states that processing of the personal data of a minor can only be based on their consent when the minor is over the age of 14.

Therefore, this is a necessary, though not moralising, book that endeavours to find answers about the complex relationship between young people and the digital world through an ambitious, innovative methodology. Ethnography and its innovative by-products, such as storytelling (Lambert & Hessler, 2018), must be advocated with regard to minors. Sometimes ethnographic conventionalism is insufficient and field agents are needed to develop the "art of telling stories," which is a resource we have found to be incredibly useful when working with minors. Through stories, we can connect to their imaginations, emotions, and projections. In other words, switching roles enables the young person to express things that are painful, complex, or worrisome. For this reason, a painstaking commitment to ethical and regulatory compliance is required, and our book addresses this as well.

We hope that reading it encourages your reflection.

Notes

1 Project registration code at the Office for the Transfer of Research Results (OTRI) of Universidad Europea de Madrid.
2 Code assigned by the Universidad Europea de Madrid Research Ethics Committee, having validated that the research meets ethical criteria.
3 Project registration code at the Office for the Transfer of Research Results (OTRI) of Universidad Europea de Madrid.
4 Code assigned by the Universidad Europea de Madrid Research Ethics Committee, having validated that the research meets ethical criteria.
5 Perceptions of Security and Risk Attitudes in "Millennials" related to the Use of Sexual/Affective Digital Apps. Enrrolla2 (2018/UEM34 – CIPI/18/070).

References

Creswell, J. (2015). *Educational research: Planning, conducting, and evaluating quantitative and qualitative research*. Pearson.

Cordero, R., Silva, A., Pérez, J., & Gómez, F. (2021). *El challenge-based research (CBR) como reto pedagógico. La investigación en criminología llevada a la docencia*. Aula Magna Proyecto Clave McGraw Hill.

García-Ruiz, M. E., & Lena-Acebo, F. J. (2018). Aplicación del método delphi en el diseño de una investigación cuantitativa sobre el fenómeno FABLAB. *Empiria, Revista de Metodología de las Ciencias Sociales* (40), 129–166.

Franzke, A. S., Bechmann, A., Zimmer, M., & Ess, C. M. (2020). *Internet research: Ethical guidelines 3.0*. https://aoir.org/reports/ethics3.pdf.

Haraway, D. (1990). *Simians, cyborgs, and women: The reinvention of nature*. Routledge. https://doi.org/10.4324/9780203873106.

Hall, S., & Winlow, S. (2020). Ultra-realismo. In G. Ríos & A. Silva (Eds.), *Nuevos horizontes en la investigación criminológica. Ultra-realismo* (pp. 5–24). Universidad de San Martín de Porres.

Khatcherian, E., Zullino, D., De Leo, D., & Achab, S. (2012). Feelings of loneliness: Understanding the risk of suicidal ideation in adolescents with internet addiction. A theoretical model to answer to a systematic literature review, without results. *International Journal of Environmental Research and Public Health* 19(4), 2012. doi:10.3390/ijerph19042012.

Lambert, J., & Hessler, B. (2018). *Digital storytelling: Capturing lives, creating community*. Routledge.

Observatorio Nacional de Tecnología y Sociedad. (2022). *Beneficios y riesgos del uso de Internet y las redes sociales. 2022.* Ministerio de Asuntos Económicos y Transformación Digital. https://www.ontsi.es/sites/ontsi/files/2022-02/beneficios_y_riesgos_uso_de_internet_y_redessociales_2022.pdf.

Raymen, T. (2020). El enigma del daño social y la barrera del liberalismo: Por qué la zemiología necesita una teoría del bien. In G. Ríos & A. Silva (Eds.), *Nuevos horizontes en la investigación criminológica. Ultra-Realismo* (pp. 25–52). Universidad de San Martín de Porres.

Silva, A. (2024). Dando forma a las sombras. Comprendiendo la construcción del conocimiento y el dispositivo encubierto en las etnografías del Ultra-Realismo [doctoral dissertation, UNED]. http://e-spacio.uned.es/fez/view/tesisuned:ED-Pg-DivSubSoc-Asilva

Silva, A., & Pérez, J. R. (2020). *Criminología de frontera. Una propuesta crítica a la Criminología española.* Eolas.

2 Fatal system error

Current structural problems in academia

2.1. The issue of educational capitalism

Postmodern education (Lyotard, 2006) is the result of the interference of the neoliberal model in education, where humanistic ideals are colonised by technological and economistic principles. Slaughter and Leslie (1997) pointed this out when they coined the term "academic capitalism." The neoliberal economic model, which was based on the "idea that public services, such as education, were inefficient for society and costly for governments" (Briggs et al., 2018, p. 4), eventually spread to every sphere of political life, including education (Bauman & Donskis, 2015).

This market-centric model poses a threat to the "validity, coherence and rethinking of the university as an institution and the degrees taught there" (Cordero, 2017, p. 72). According to Freire (2017, cited in Ortiz & Zacarías, 2020), nowadays "educational practice is a neoliberal pragmatism in which educating has been reduced to training but not teaching" (p. 11).

Research by Slaughter and Leslie (1997) even back in the 1990s showed the presence of academic capitalism in the United States, Canada, Australia, and the United Kingdom, as well as its prevalence in Latin America. This model was already established internationally when the COVID-19 crisis offered the perfect excuse for its ultimate launch through the expansion of digital capitalism (Jarquín & Díez, 2022) in which "the technology-based multinationals GAFAM [Google, Apple, Facebook, Amazon and Microsoft] consolidated their offering of educational services in the Global Educational Industry" (p. 240). These services are purchased by educational

DOI: 10.4324/9781003399315-2

institutions for the alleged purpose of facilitating teaching and learning tasks, exposing the entire educational community to the risks and
designs of the major platforms, which, as private stakeholders, have
"specific political and commercial interests and goals" (Jarquín &
Díez, 2022, p. 240).

Just as economic globalisation has reached most of the countries
in the world, the economics of knowledge (Bermejo, 2015) has been
established across every continent. Both capitalism and globalisation
introduce a quantifiable, technical, and productive dimension in
educational processes (Barone & Martínez-Gómez, 2001), generating an intensive use of knowledge (Tedesco, 2002) that ends up
devaluing and undermining it.

In fact, according to Tedesco (2002), two of the educational
milestones reached over the past two centuries – social mobility and
democratisation – have been eroded by the dominant class for the
benefit of their capitalistic interests. Today, unlike in the past, getting an education does not lead to social improvement. The increase
in the number of university graduates decreases their opportunities,
giving rise to what Thorpe (2008) called the "opportunity trap,"
intensifying competition among graduates and forcing them to
accept highly precarious conditions in order to get into the workplace (Standing, 2011).

By removing from academic learning the added value entailed in
social growth and distinction from one's original class, learning
becomes instrumentalised, returning to the aforementioned productive dimension of education (Barone & Martínez-Gómez, 2001)
while the acquisition of culture is relegated to the background.

Likewise, the democratisation of education, understood as a universal right (Vidal, 2012), has gradually weakened, especially because,
as Barone and Martínez-Gómez (2001) noted, the commercial logic
behind academic postmodernity has moved toward the privatisation
of educational fields. The catalyst of this process has been a compendium of ridiculous political postulates. Through diverse claims,
this ideology has gradually caught on among the public, and the
latter, in exercising their right to vote, has made it a reality. According to Miñana and Rodríguez (2003), the message conveyed is that

> relationships between public and private are better defined by the
> market and freedom to choose than by a State operating out of a

supposed "public interest." That which is private is superior, morally and operationally speaking, than State or public options.

(p. 8)

Advocating the private and state-funded charter education model as an assurance of better management, administration, and education (Ortega, 2003) and assuming that the public educational sector is incapable of meeting the educational needs demanded by society is misleading to a certain extent. On a sociopolitical level, every effort should be made to ensure that it is precisely the public education system that, at all levels, guarantees adequate and competitive schooling that is universal and inclusive. And even though this is possible and necessary, political praxis strays from these principles, since "the educational process in the neoliberal capitalist system is designed to exclude those who do not meet the requirements of human capital prescribed by the economic dimension" (Ortiz & Zacarías, 2020, p. 14). It should be noted that this exclusion is driven by numerous factors: functional diversity, gender, age, race, ethnicity, and so forth. Thus, we are dealing with an extraordinary manoeuvre executed by the dominant elite, which cancels out community action and the public sphere (Habermas, 1999). As such, given that part of the population is excluded from education due to a lack of resources, we can classify this action as structural violence (Galtung, 1998).

2.2. The issue of commercialisation of knowledge

When, at the end of the last century, Slaughter and Leslie (1997) referred to academic capitalism as the outcome of applying market logic to university and research institutions, it became clear that states, policies, researchers, and so forth had been aligned to serve the market, putting a price on knowledge. This is no trivial matter because it amounts to funding those research projects from which the greatest profits could be gleaned (Bermejo, 2015). Such a practice would bar virtually any research projects focusing on the "most vulnerable." We must recall that if the capitalist system suffers from anything, it is that it turns away from the community. Capitalism is interested in the individualised mass eager to consume (Baudrillard, 2009).

However, academic capitalism not only decides which research is to be funded but also which researchers are to be hired (Slaughter & Leslie, 1997), interested only in those that manage to attract external funding, which in turn can only be achieved from a perspective of politeness or a system need (Silva, 2019). This entails promoting positivist research while greatly complicating research of a qualitative nature focusing mainly on ethnography. The reason for this is that, firstly, this latter type takes more time to attain data and, secondly, because it furnishes in-depth knowledge of the problem, which could be "uncomfortable" for the dominant powers. According to Abad and Dávila (2020),

> the prevailing epistemic and temporal logic of research under academic capitalism is imposed as the only possible option from the perspective of efficiency, calculability and predictability.
>
> (p. 92)

We are talking about two opposing ways of gaining knowledge from higher education institutions: 1) the public system of knowledge/learning (Habermas, 1999) and 2) the capitalist system of knowledge/learning (Slaughter & Rhoades, 2004).

Here at the Knowledge and Research Group on Social Problems (henceforth referred to as GCIPS, its Spanish acronym), we demand that knowledge be returned to the public space, not only as a right but also as a social need. Academia must offer solutions to all social issues, regardless of whether they have the market's blessing. To do this, a new approach to traditional research methodologies must be taken, adapting them to new social realities (e.g., the digital world). Berry (2011), for example, proposes a "computational turn," which González and Servín (2017) define as a "hybrid approach in which computational techniques are used in order to go from an initial impulse toward quantitative research to another that is qualitative, critical and generative" (p. 62). There is a need for research techniques adapted to the new realities, using an experimental, qualitative research methodology, especially an ethnographic or digital ethnographic approach (Pink et al., 2016). At the GCIPS, we feel that mixed methods (Silva & Pérez, 2020) are essential for analysing society today, given its complexity. These methods integrate both quantitative and qualitative perspectives into the research to give depth to the analysis.

Table 2.1 Comparison of the public and private knowledge management models

PUBLIC SYSTEM OF KNOWL-EDGE/LEARNING	CAPITALIST SYSTEM OF KNOWLEDGE/LEARNING
Knowledge is public and a civil right.	Knowledge is a private asset that can be traded for individual gain.
Governed by universal humanistic principles of research: ethics, community benefit, universality, and free circulation of knowledge.	Academic institutions and their allies take priority over knowledge. Knowledge generation depends on profits.
Scholars are free to exercise their duties as teachers and researchers.	Freedom of knowledge is replaced by market interests.
Researchers have the right and freedom to focus their interests wherever they see fit. General interest is prioritised over market logic.	Knowledge ceases to be circular. Scholars are controlled by an institution, which decides what to do with their findings.
Knowledge is considered circular and necessary, serving the community and benefiting the public.	Knowledge has little value; what really matters is how it can be used in trade.
Research emerges separately from governmental or corporate interests.	Priority is given to knowledge that benefits market interests, such as high technology.
There is no bond between public and private.	The merging of the public and private spheres is the foundation for the science and knowledge trade.
As negative aspects, academic and research freedom can be used for purposes that are contrary to public interest.	As negative aspects, knowledge is transformed into something exclusive, with monetary value. The social mass lacks sufficient financial resources to gain access to it. This circumstance leads to intellectual poverty, knowledge gaps, and hindered creativity.

Source: Compiled by the authors based on Slaughter and Rhoades (2004) and Brunner et al. (2019).

Little remains of the university as a space for independent knowledge and wisdom. Autonomy in decision-making has been left in the hands of financial returns (Slaughter & Leslie, 2001). To put it crudely, if it sells, it can be done, otherwise it cannot be done.

It is not easy to elude the pressures of the academic market. Research comes at a high cost in terms of human and material capital. Researchers must decide between conducting research that they can "live by" or playing the system's game and "living" besides doing research. Those of us who believe that research is a necessary, ethical praxis that must contribute value to society endeavour to increase our autonomy. To do this, we seek other sources of collaboration and/or funding outside the usual channels, even though we have been aware from the outset that this attitude will prompt a confrontation with the establishment and we accept that it will be harder to publish our research in high-impact journals.[1]

2.3. The issue of course programmes designed by business

The entry into force of the Bologna Declaration (Bologna Plan) on 19 June 1999 is a clear example of the spread of academic capitalism across Europe. In the end, the plan was implemented in 2010 with the creation of the European Higher Education Area (EHEA) in which there was a move toward standardisation of university studies with the complicity of business under the umbrella of employability. For Díez (2011),

> this reform does not seem to be aimed at placing the university at society's service to make it more just, wiser, more universal, more equitable, more understanding, but rather at adapting the university to the market, a very specific part of society, whose aims are not focused precisely on justice, comprehension or equity.
>
> (p. 59)

The biggest criticism of the Bologna Declaration was doubtless the commercialisation of the university and the strong support for university privatisation. According to data from the CRUE,[2] the number of private universities in Spain has multiplied fivefold since 1995, going from 7 to 34. This trend is also seen elsewhere in Europe, where charter universities have emerged in large numbers in countries like Finland, Belgium, and Lithuania (Eurostat, 2021).

The increase in private or charter education offerings has prompted a significant increase in the number of students that choose private learning. They see it as an assurance of employability. The data confirm this idea, as the employment rate for individuals that attended private universities is 5.4% higher than at public universities (INE, 2020, p. 2).

Market logic creates sellable degrees that are accepted by business, which may spell the end of one of the basic principles of university learning – critical thinking. According to Ruíz (2010), the educational function of school (also transferrable to the university)

> requires that both the teaching and student bodies have sufficient intellectual independence to maintain a critical attitude toward socialising influences and to resist and recreate.
>
> (p. 184)

This independence is in no way guaranteed, thus also affecting the development of critical thinking, if the teachers themselves have decided to accept without any criticism whatsoever a model that prioritises competences and skills over knowledge, as Bologna proposes for Europe as a whole. Bermejo (2015) sees this as an effort to reformulate education without a critical spirit. For some time now, education has been based on empty concepts on an educational level but with enormous returns for business: effectiveness, excellence, productivity, and so forth.

The situation in Latin America is similar because, although these countries have different resources, the North American role model and the birth of dual university training in Mexico, Colombia, Ecuador, and Guatemala have placed the university at the service of business (Ibarra, 2003). This circumstance was confirmed by Brunner et al. (2021) following a review of the theories of Slaughter and Leslie (1997) with a view to ascertaining whether the academic capitalism they had observed in Latin America remained true 20 years later. After diverse analyses in several countries, Brunner and colleagues concluded that this phenomenon was present in Latin America despite the unique features of the different countries on the continent.

The observable consequences of the commercialisation of knowledge in Latin America do not differ greatly from those of English-speaking or European countries. Take Brazil, for example, where there is once again evidence of the coexistence of public and private models (Brunner et al., 2021):

A public system featuring its unique political and bureaucratic *ethos* compared to a private system that, while it contains capitalist strategies for garnering resources, lacks academic density, favouring the sale of low-cost courses and qualifications through the extensive use of administration technologies and transmission of contents.

(p. 12)

2.4. The issue of bureaucratised meritocracy

Another requirement of academic capitalism is the return of prestige and money that comes from papers, which Bermejo (2015) refers to as "papernomics." This control system extends to academic life and to the "process of creating scientific knowledge" (p. 130), forcing researchers to publish or even pay for many scientific articles and trapping them in a "wonderful publishing business" (p. 131). Research lecturers live under constant pressure to improve their publication ratios, a stressful and demanding spiral known as "publish or perish" (Moosa, 2018).

This circumstance was already observed two decades earlier by Gibbons et al. (1994), who talked about how researchers had been devoured by a huge machine that produced knowledge in the form of scientific articles.

Global production of scientific articles around the world is on the rise. In 2019, it was 21% above (UNESCO, 2021) the 3,000,000 per year in 2015 (Bermejo, 2015). However, this does not mean that the growth has been positive. Researchers, as well as teachers, are forced to produce tirelessly if they intend to have an active, developing academic career (Silva, 2019). They cannot rebel against a bureaucracy-laden meritocratic machine because their jobs depend on that system.

Instead of providing researchers with resources to facilitate their work, the postmodern educational model has imposed a doctrine of "do it yourself" (Cordero, 2017, p. 72). According to Bauman and Donskis (2015), this academic setting requires teachers to be versatile:

Be a scholar, essayist and publisher all at once. Raise the money for your research, lead it, publish a monograph and then launch a public relations campaign to promote it.

(p. 166)

All these roles must be played by scholars in order to achieve an alleged "excellence" so that they are not expelled from the system. However, this multiplicity of tasks is totally contrary to the pace required in research: slow, deliberate, and certain to reach a profound level of thought from which to obtain valid conclusions. In postmodern times, knowledge is truncated at the surface, dematerialising reality (Lyotard, 2006).

This system of merits[3] is the paradigm of socially legitimised individualism. Indeed, Bauman and Donskis (2015) see it as "a sort of technocratic and bureaucratic tyranny imposed in the name of freedom and progress" (p. 173).

2.5.   The issue of the customer that studies

Educational economics has turned students into customers (Hall, 2015). This new paradigm breaks away from the classic student-teacher relationship. Students-turned-customers purchase a service and make use of the part that interests them; in fact, they believe the teacher is there to serve them as part of the service they have purchased. The customers acquire the knowledge not as a vital learning experience that will accompany them for the rest of their lives but as a sporadic need that can be discarded when the time comes. This is especially true when the academic model of university degrees aims to provide competences and skills that will be required of future graduates in the course of their professional activity (Cordero, 2017). In other words, they are not looking for people who stand out from the rest but rather individuals who perpetuate certain ways of working in connivance with business.

Universities, converted into commercial pseudo-entities (Briggs et al., 2018), have been forced to prove that they are productive (Hall, 2015) and that they are satisfactory to external customers (the students), using consultation instruments to discern their opinions about a certain professor and about the institution (Silva, 2019).

Teacher and academic satisfaction surveys are used as a penalty system for teachers (their wage increases and even their longevity at the institution are based on them) as well as a source of information in the effort to distinguish themselves from competing brands (other universities).

In sum, we are confronted with a kind of utilitarianism applied to knowledge by the customer/student, which strips the teacher of respect, no longer serving as a role model but as a mediator, "a new way of conceiving educational relationships between students and teachers" (Paricio, 2017, p. 7).

This new relational paradigm (mediator-customer) renders the learning process increasingly complex. Students, who are focused on earning degrees and getting a good job that offers them lucrative benefits, confront knowledge and learning with no motivation, patience, or empathy, the last of which is essential to have a positive impact on society through their future professional development.

In criminology studies, for example, the lack of student motivation becomes especially relevant in courses that focus on research methodologies, for three reasons:

1   Short-term thinking: The values of consumer society (Baudrillard, 2009), characterised by everything "fast" – fast fashion, fast food, fast love (Cordero, Pérez, et al., 2021), etc. – have led to fast learning, which is incompatible with the deliberate, thoughtful, and patient pace of research.
2   Hyper-narcissistic hyper-individualism (Lipovetsky, 2016): As a social phenomenon characteristic of a light society (Lipovetsky, 2016) that removes the individual from the collective. This generates a change in the priority order in which individual interest is put before general interest.
3   The disconnection from tangible reality, which makes students deal with research as if it were a game, without understanding how important it is in transformation, social change, and potential victimisation stemming from misconduct.

At the same time, Silva and Pérez (2020) highlight the lack of methodological training in Spanish criminology degrees (as well as the preponderance of the quantitative). Inequalities are also found among the different types of universities (public, private, and religious).

At GCIPS, we have found that this situation can be reversed through the use of innovative educational methodologies such as challenge-based research (CBR; Cordero, Silva, et al., 2021), for example, "experimental learning based on challenges" (Cordero, Silva, et al., 2021), which turns students into an active part of the research process by means of an immersive pedagogical challenge based on mixed methods that is open to dialogue, intimate and realistic. Annex 1 shows the sequential methodological design of CBR as an inspirational resource for other research lecturers.

CBR is a guided methodological approach in which teachers show students that they are capable of following the research path. At the same time, it helps them understand that applied criminology (or any social science) is a means of constructing a better, more just, and more equitable society.

Experience in the application of CBR has confirmed that as students discover their research skills, they become empowered as researchers and end up feeling better prepared to carry out their future professional activities in a profession that requires them to get involved and understand the collective.

Furthermore, promoting the transfer of the knowledge acquired by the students in their research leads them to become more committed to the course and to take a more mature stance in the development of projects. They are aware that it is not a game.

In conclusion, today's students will only be able to become agents of change and social transformation tomorrow if we introduce knowledge and society to them in the form of critical, reflexive, and practical learning free of taboos.

Notes

1 We are referring here to the concept of "publication bias" (Bermejo, 2015, p. 131) in which papers that break with or challenge basic ideas in a field end up becoming virtually unpublishable, unlike others that contain an aggregate set of data and are easily admitted.
2 Spanish University Rectors' Conference. This organisation represents a total of 76 public and private Spanish universities and serves as the liaison between these institutions and the central government.
3 Consisting in accumulating points by publishing articles, years of teaching experience, visits abroad, research projects, and so forth in order to take part in the teaching career.

References

Abad, B., & Dávila, A. (2020). Misfortune of qualitative social research in the times of academic capitalism. *New Trends in Qualitative Research*, 4, 82–95. https://doi.org/10.36367/ntqr.4.2020.82-95.

Barone, M., & Martínez-Gómez, R. (2001). Globalización y posmodernidad. Encrucijada para las políticas sociales del nuevo milenio. *Papeles*, 74, 9–16.

Baudrillard, J. (2009). *La sociedad del consumo*. Siglo XXI Editores.

Bauman, Z., & Donskis, L. (2015). *Ceguera moral. La pérdida de la sensibilidad en la modernidad líquida*. Paidós.

Bermejo, J. C. (2015). *La tentación del rey Midas. Para una economía política del conocimiento*. Siglo XXI Editores.

Berry, D. (Ed.). (2011). *The computational turn. Understanding digital humanities*. Sage.

Briggs, D., Pérez, J. R., & Cordero, R. (2018). From crime science to the crime of science . *Safer Communities*, 1(17), 22–32.

Brunner, J. J., Labrana, J., Ganga, F., & Rodríguez-Ponce, E. (2019). Circulation and reception of the theory of "academic capitalism" in Latin America. *Education Policy Analysis Archives*, 27, 79. https://doi.org/10.14507/epaa.27.4368.

Brunner, J. J., Salmi, J., & Labraña, J. (2021). *Enfoques de sociología y economía política de la educación superior: Aproximaciones al capitalismo académico en América Latina*. Ediciones Universidad Diego Portales.

Cordero, R. (2017). La cosificación educativa posmoderna y su impacto en los estudios de criminología en España. *Criminología y Justicia*, 2(3), 65–81.

Cordero, R., Pérez, J. R., & Silva, A. (2021). La gestión del deseo afectivo-sexual en la crisis del COVID-19. In E. Del Campo (Ed.), *La vida cotidiana en tiempos de la COVID. Una antropología de la pandemia* (pp. 201–225). Catarata.

Cordero, R., Silva, A., Pérez, J. R., & Gómez, F. (2021). *El challenge based research (CBR) como reto pedagógico. La investigación en criminología llevada a la docencia*. McGraw Hill.

Díez, E. J. (2011). La McDonalización de la educación superior. *Revista Interuniversitaria de Formación del Profesorado*, 25(3), 59–76.

Eurostat. (2021). *Students enrolled in tertiary education by education level, programme orientation, sex, type of institution and intensity of participation*. https://ec.europa.eu/eurostat/databrowser/view/EDUC_UOE_ENRT01.

Galtung, J. (1998). *Tras la violencia, 3R - reconstrucción, reconciliación, resolución: Afrontando los efectos visibles e invisibles de la guerra y la violencia*. Bakeaz.

Gibbons, M., Limoges, C., Nowotny, H., Schwartzman, S., Scott, P., & Trow, M. (1994). *La nueva producción del conocimiento*. Pomares-Corredor.

González, L. J., & Servín, A. (2017). Métodos cualitativos digitales. Un acercamiento a la antropología digital y otras posturas de investigación online. *Virtualis: Revista de Cultura Digital*, 8(15), 61–80.

Habermas, J. (1999). *Teoría de la acción comunicativa: Racionalidad de la acción*. Taurus.

Hall, G. (2015, October 18). Does Academia.edu mean open access is becoming irrelevant? *Media Gifts*. http://www.garyhall.info/journal/2015/10/18/doesacademiaedu-mean-open-access-is-becoming-irrelevant.html.

Ibarra. E. (2003). Capitalismo académico y globalización: La universidad reinventada. *Educação & Sociedade*, 24(84). https://doi.org/10.1590/S0101-73302003000300017.

INE. (2020). *Encuesta de inserción laboral de titulados universitarios año 2019*. Instituto Nacional de Estadística.

Jarquín, M. R., & Díez, E. J. (2022). Google en Iberoamérica: Expansión corporativa y capitalismo digital en educación. *Revista Española de Educación Comparada*, 42, 240–260. https://doi.org/10.5944/reec.42.2023.34322.

Lipovetsky, G. (2016). *De la ligereza*. Anagrama.

Lyotard, J. F. (2006). *La condición posmoderna*. Cátedra.

Miñana, C., & Rodríguez, J. G. (2003). La educación en el contexto neo-liberal. In D. I. Restrepo (Ed.), *La falacia neoliberal. Crítica y alternativas* (pp. 285–321). Universidad Nacional de Colombia.

Moosa, I. A. (2018). *Publish or perish: Perceived benefits versus unintended consequences*. Edward Elgar.

Ortega, M. A. (2003). Privatización y ¿eficiencia económica? *Gestión y Política Pública*, 12(2), 207–239.

Ortiz, M., & Zacarías, M. (2020). La inclusión educativa en el sistema neoliberal capitalista. *IE Revista de Investigación Educativa de la REDIECH*, 11, e794. doi:10.33010/ie_rie_rediech.v11i0.794.

Paricio, J. (2017). El estudiante como cliente: Un cambio de paradigma en la educación superior. *Debats. Revista de Cultura, Poder y Sociedad*, 131(2), 41–55. http://doi.org/10.28939/iam.debats.131-2.4.

Pink, S., Horst, H., Postill, J., Hjorth, L., Lewis, T., & Tacchi, J. (2016). *Digital ethnography: Principles and practice*. Sage.

Ruiz Román, C. (2010). La educación en la sociedad postmoderna: Desafíos y oportunidades. *Revista Complutense de Educación*, 21(1), 173–188.

Silva, A. (2019). Etnografía [des]encubierta. Una mirada a la práctica etnográfica encubierta del Ultra Realismo criminológico [unpublished master's thesis]. UNED.

Silva, A., & Pérez, J. R. (2020). *Criminología de frontera. Una propuesta crítica a la Criminología española*. Eolas.

Slaughter, S., & Leslie, L. L. (1997). *Academic capitalism: Politics, policies, and the entrepreneurial university*. Johns Hopkins University Press.

Slaughter, S., & Leslie, L. L. (2001). Expanding and elaborating the concept of academic capitalism. *Organization*, 8(2), 154–161.

Slaughter, S., & Rhoades, G. (2004). *Academic capitalism and the new economy: Markets, state, and higher education*. Johns Hopkins University Press.

Standing, G. (2011). *The precariat: The new dangerous class*. Bloomsbury.

Tedesco, J. C. (2002). La educación en el marco del nuevo capitalismo. *Revista IIDH*, 36, 131–147.

Thorpe, C. (2008). Capitalism, audit and the demise of the humanistic academy. *Workplace: A Journal for Academic Labor*, 15, 103–125.

UNESCO. (2021). *La carrera contra el reloj para un desarrollo más inteligente. Informe de la UNESCO sobre la Ciencia 2021*. UNESCO.

Vidal, V. M. (2012). Redefiniciones en el papel del estado: La privatización de lo público y las implicaciones para la democratización de la educación. *Revista de Currículum y Formación del Profesorado*, 16(3), 191–211.

3 Terms of service
The ethics of working with children online

3.1. Ethics and morals in criminological research

To start this chapter, we need to define the concepts of ethics and morals. There is a tendency to believe that everyone understands this matter. However, in practice, the line between ethical and moral stances begins to blur. Some of the structural problems discussed in the previous chapter have ultimately led many researchers toward ethics understood in terms of individualism. In light of the need to safeguard their career and interests in the academic setting they work in, it is clear how academic capitalism can influence researchers' ethical perspective. This is evident when there is an attempt to ignore possible ethical dilemmas by treating subjects universally, choosing quick, economical research projects with a positivist approach and geared toward market demands. The issue becomes more pronounced when we see that the regulatory frameworks for ethics are not aligned with our fields of study. Regulatory ethics is too bureaucratic and prone to simple, rigid generalisations. In short, the field of study is viewed as an aseptic setting in which all the variables are under control. However, criminologists do not do research in laboratories, and we cannot foresee every action that is going to occur during our research. Instead, we work with uncertainty and adaptation. We must not adhere to such an individualistic proposal because "if everything is based on mere personal morals and everyone's is different" (Díaz de Rada, 2010, p. 68), an alignment is impossible. Therefore, this is where dialogues start to emerge between what is moral and what is ethical, or which of the two is more important.

DOI: 10.4324/9781003399315-3

If we search the literature in the analytical category of "ethics," the results found are paradoxical. Some authors link ethics to moral thinking and morals to experiences (Ojeda de López et al., 2007, p. 349), while organisations like the CSIC (2022) relate ethics to an interest in considering ethical aspects of research, their nature and aim. Even the dictionary links ethics to morals, indicating that it is a "set of moral rules that govern a person's conduct in any area of life" (Real Academia de la Lengua Española, 2024). Despite the semantic anomia seen above, we can assert that they all have a gradual common aim, which is to ensure that a benefit considered excellent is obtained and that this is achieved through a set of practices that are accepted or assumed to be correct by the community. However, what is excellent? Is there friction between the aims and the means? Does anyone have sufficient capacity to dictate what is correct or what is reprehensible in every context?

In short, the issue of morals and ethics raises enough concerns to cause an urge to relegate it to oblivion. We shall use an excerpt from Mèlich (2010) to give us an initial approach to the difference between these two terms:

> This positioning oneself in the world is life. But the human condition consists precisely in a mismatch. While morality is part of the world, ethics comes with eccentricity, this failure to fit. If morals stem from the world, ethics stem from life. Therefore, if the world and life were the same, then ethics would make no sense. If ethics exists, it is because what exists, exists and "something else," what "is not yet," what is not even imaginable, what is to come, the expectation of the event, of an impossible event.
>
> (p. 320)

In other words, ethics is not a regulatory framework but a response. Ethics and morals cannot be taken as the same thing because the former comes from the division of the latter when an action takes place in the field that is not controlled or foreseeable. To sum up, according to Mèlich, morals would be a regulatory framework that is not generally expressed in writing but does operate via rules. Ethics, on the other hand, would be understood as the sum of the responses that surpass those frameworks. To extrapolate, this means that deontological codes would, in practice, be moral codes, and the responses developed by each researcher in the field are what link them to ethics.

By following the tendency to link the question of "what should I do?" to ethics, the error is repeated infinitely because ethics seen in this way would operate on the basis of Kantian principles (Kant, 2005, 2013). This is the stance taken by most of our institutions that regulate ethics and where the underlying problem that must be highlighted lies. The Kantian thesis is an extremely aseptic proposal that aims to work on the premise that there are laws that are universally accepted by everyone autonomously (Aramayo, 1999, p. 24). Neither Kant nor our regulatory agencies thought to reflect on each subject's capacity for agency and their right to dissent. Therefore, in the field, we see a reflection of the weaknesses in Kant's proposal – that is, that their application beyond the theoretical realm is smashed to pieces (Aramayo, 1999, pp. 25–27). How can this matter be solved? Mèlich (2010, p. 317) proposed drawing a dividing line between morals resembling Kantian principles and more liberated ethics that can work in more changing contexts. One example of how this is applied can be seen in this field journal excerpt:

> It doesn't work, in my opinion this makes no sense at all. They make me use an informed consent in a public, digital field where I will not be in contact with anyone. If I were in a public park, it would be the same and they wouldn't demand this, the disparity between regulations and implementation is supreme. Cultural norms in this field are an oxymoron, it is visualising all the content without interacting beyond a mere like. I have sent several consent forms by private messaging and none have been answered. Instead, in the description of my account, I wrote that I am a researcher and that research is being done, next to a link to a website that gives more information about the project. Legally speaking, this is the most ethical I can aspire to be in a context like this.
>
> (Field journal excerpt, Antonio Silva)

As we can see, the field agents strive to continue obeying the law but making adjustments for the setting in which we are working. This self-critical reflection, which we perhaps find hard to accept or which may even prompt us to be more concerned in the field because we are exposed to contradictions, to tensions between the desk and the field, and so forth, is crucial. This is the case because it creates a starting point: accepting that we can never be absolutely ethical. This is impossible for a very pragmatic reason, which is that ethics provides a disparate solution to each unexpected problem that crops up in the field but does not answer whether that is what we should have done; such a response would then be linked to morals (Mèlich, 2010, p. 320).

3.1.1. Ethics committees

Having discussed this matter, it is also necessary to look at our ethics-regulating organisations, the ethics committees. The questioning of these entities is nothing new, nor has it been ignored in the social sciences (Silva, 2019, p. 68). The most significant criticism is related to its very aetiology, its emergence within the biomedical context, given that the consequence of this has been a painful disjointedness with social research (Schrag, 2010). In light of the above, it is relevant to take a moment to contemplate whether the inheritance of these biomedical principles in parts of the social sciences is influenced by the classic nature-society duality (Latour, 2007) or by the terror that seems to pervade certain sectors of the social sciences of not being considered "proper" scientists.

At any rate, as we have held from the beginning, in the social sciences in general, and in criminology in particular, it is rare for one plus one to be two (Steenhout, 2013, pp. 190–191). Attempting to operate with the methodological monism from centuries ago, adopting the lens of natural sciences to understand today's social phenomena will bring nothing more than the creation of a crude and unreal portrayal of the phenomenon studied (Katz, 2006, p. 500; Murphy & Dingwall, 2007, p. 2231; Schrag, 2010; Stark, 2012). This reductionism of an experimental nature is very dangerous, especially for tasks related to ethnography (Lederman, 2006, p. 487). Let us consider the rise in ethics committees (Bernuz et al., 2019, p. 41) and the subjugation they could exert by means of controls and audits. This could be highly beneficial if the rules of the game were adapted to our fields of study, but the problem is that this is not the case, as we have seen in the excerpt from the field journal above.

So we find that a direct consequence is that an organisation that should assure adherence to moral codes and ethics in the field ends up playing the leading role in the theatre of "biasing research projects," where tickets are only sold for certain methods and phenomena while the rest are excluded.

When this particular theatre piece begins, there are collateral repercussions. Two types of research are portrayed: true research and fringe research. Indeed, we return to the dualities, exalting positivist, quick, economical, and superficial research to the detriment of research that does not march so easily to the drum of the academic capitalism structure. In short, we are confronted with a sharp misalignment between ethics committees and the social sciences, which is particularly acute when it comes to criminology and ethnography.

However, it could diminish our credibility to establish this dialogue with the reader without giving examples applied to our research. Therefore, we will address two key elements: a) private versus public and b) informed consent.

3.1.2. Codes of ethics, conception of public versus private space, and informed consent

Why have we chosen the private-public duality as the first key element? Basically, because it has proven to be an ethically complex correlative in our research on children in digital environments. Sometimes it seems quite clear what is private and what is public: Is Instagram public or private? You are probably feeling quite proud of yourself when you assert that it is public and that accounts may or may not be, depending on how their owners have set them up. If only everything were that easy. In fact, as you may have expected, the issue of how the private and public realms are defined directly affects our work as researchers, given that we may be conducting a covert ethnography (Calvey, 2017).

Before going in depth, we would like to note how some of the main codes of ethics conceive public and/or private spaces in cyberspace.[1] We shall focus on the following:

- *American Anthropological Association (AAA)*: This organisation did not address the matter thoroughly. In fact, the committee discussed the matter in response to a consultation as to whether there was a formal policy on ethical research practice in social media, and the answer was that no such policy existed (American Anthropological Association, 2023).

- *American Sociological Association (ASA)*: In reference to cyberspace, the ASA's Section 10.5.c states that "assurance of confidentiality is not required in the case of information available from public records or unrestricted internet sites." Then, as indicated in Section 11.1.a, "not all information on the internet is considered public, and must include informed consent procedures for research in restricted internet locations." Finally, Section 11.1.d informs us that "sociologists do not typically need informed consent when using information from public internet sites. These might include much of the content on the internet, including blogs and social media sites." In sum, cyberspace is public unless we need permission to enter a site, in which case, we must use informed consent.
- *European Commission. Ethics in Social Science and Humanities*: Indirectly, the European Commission tells us that observation in public settings does not require consent as long as it is done anonymously, discreetly, and in settings where the field agents can reasonably expect to be observed by others.
- *Association of Internet Researchers (AoIR)*: Here, they do go more in depth in their reports. Thus, in IRE 2.0 (2012), the public-private duality starts to be problematized, given that people may perform actions in public spaces under the perception or expectation of relative privacy. In other words, they may understand that their actions or remarks are public but not agree with them being used by third parties. In fact, the report goes so far as to declare that the dichotomy between public and private is no longer true in everyday life and much less so in cyberspace, where the scenario is ever changing and there is no absolute consensus on anything. In later reports, such as IRE 3.0 (2019), they even talk about quasi-public spaces to refer to spaces that are public but require a password, profile, and so on. (See how the Instagram question was not so easy?)

After reading the stances of these organisations, what we can perceive might be called anomia, dissent, or confusion regarding what is public and what is private in cyberspace. Several authors have already pointed out the lack of attention paid to ethical questions in social research in cyberspace or even the absence of codes of ethics in this regard in some countries (Estalella & Ardèvol, 2007, 2011; Gómez, 2008; Márquez, 2014; Airoldi, 2018; Lehner-Mear, 2019). In our opinion, the most coherent and best adapted position is undoubtedly that of the AoIR. This organisation encourages us to ponder a situated position, rather than one seen from outside or from above; we are encouraged to bear in mind the agent's perception of their communication and their content.

Thus, instead of merely deducing that TikTok is a public space where videos are uploaded that I can use to study, we need to understand whether the rules governing that specific field allow this action, and if we are not sure, we need to ask humbly.

Let us take, for example, a forum in which membership is required for access. In other words, a space in which you can access all the content if you are a member, but if not, you have access to only a part of it. In this setting, no one uses their name but rather pseudonyms, meaning that a significant degree of anonymity is already in place. Is the part that I can access without being a member public? Could we make use of only that content? To start, we can use none of it. Because the content, whether more public or more private, that the authors posted was not posted for the purpose of someone using it in research. However, if we dig deeper and ask if they would mind if we used their content, we may find the unexpected consent of part of the community (Silva, 2024). We are not asserting with this example that this situation is going to occur always and in every field but rather that the key lies in asking when we have concerns.

Another example is the famous POVs (points of view).[2] Let us retrieve a field note in this regard:

> The most significant cases of insecurity, anxiety and addiction are seen in Laura and Coral. They are suffering and they say so, and the more they say it, the more the community pokes at them. There is a constant problem in not knowing whether the social media is a social network or a private environment. They sometimes share very intimate things like WhatsApp chats or recordings of themselves crying when they have anxiety attacks, weeping and moaning about breakups or pseudo-empowerment

reflections against criticism of their bodies. But then they do not admit any criticism regarding what they have shared, pointing out that the others don't know them and only see what they want them to see. This latter point is true, but the constant sensation is that besides that, they are incapable of separating what they want to show sometimes, and only snap when they feel insecure. The vicious circle or roller coaster of hormones, exposure, addiction and insecurity even lead posts to take on a recurring directionality: I'm very strong-I love myself very much-I want to be alone//we are unhealthily in love-I feel bad or melancholy content-anxiety attack//recorded weeping-telling off the community for being critical and start all over again.

(Field journal excerpt, Antonio Silva)

The second key element in this section refers to informed consent, as mentioned above. This document serves several purposes. Firstly, it is to verify that the field agents understand the research. Secondly, it is to confirm that they are able to identify both the institution and the researchers carrying out the project. Thirdly, it must be capable of clearly explaining how the field agents' data will be processed (use, dissemination, destruction, etc.) so that they know what they are being exposed to if they agree. Finally, it must safeguard anonymity and confidentiality (Bernuz et al., 2019; Díaz, 2019; Heap & Waters, 2019). In this light, it is a tool that offers the agents guarantees and rights, so it is positive.

However, there are always several ways to read a situation, and this is no exception. There are interests hiding behind informed consent (Gledhill, 2000), undermining this document to the point that it has ended up being seen as a bureaucratic obstacle of a generalised, deductive nature that does not actually solve the problems it aims to solve.

Although informed consent may be verbal Flick, 2015; Clark et al., 2021), ethics committees usually require these documents prior to starting the research for approval (Díaz, 2019). This entails two logical steps: deductive nature and delays. Regarding the first step, we are doomed to failure because it is impossible to generate a valid document for people in the field before entering the field. This means we may draft a document that quickly becomes obsolete (Díaz de Rada, 2012). Regarding the second step, we can solve the first issue by sending the informed consent forms back to the ethics committee and applying for approval again. Consequences? We may repeat this process several times in the course of the research, and the periodic meetings of the ethics committees will doom the project to failure.[3] In addition, we need to consider several important issues about the document itself:

- A generic wording to skirt the aforementioned issues is no solution.
- Informed consent must be adapted and flexible. The research goals may change and the profiles of the people we meet in a field may differ greatly.
- We are not always free (Fernández, 2010, pp. 304–305) to communicate the details of our research to the field agents.
- The consent itself may not be recognised as a tool of assurance because the field agents do not understand or obey the academic authorities (Díaz, 2019).
- It is not possible in every field to deploy ethical consent that ensures the safety of the research subject and the researcher. This is especially the case in criminology, where dangerous, clandestine phenomena are studied.

Indeed, in relation to the last two points, we must be self-critical and humble (Calvey, 2017, p. 52). Implementing informed consent does not necessarily mean that research will be developed ethically in practice, nor does a failure to implement it automatically entail malpractice (Muñoz & Salinas, 2018; Silva, 2019). We need to move beyond schizoid thinking, support a more gradual conception, and operate based on dialogic ethics (Dietz, 2011, p. 9), allowing researchers the freedom to adapt to cultural norms in the field, where a document like this sometimes is neither meaningful nor valid. Furthermore, it is our responsibility to approach consent as a tool that truly seeks to ensure the safety of the field agents and researchers instead of focusing on avoiding litigation. In sum, the consent form must have reasonable wording and be adaptable and flexible.

As an example, during the A.I.DRIANA research project, we were constrained by the intended bureaucratic rigidity when it came to informed consent. The ethics committee asked for different consent forms, one for parents and others for children. However, it should be noted that we were working with children aged 13–15. According to Spanish law, parent consent was needed for 12- and 13-year-olds, but it was not required for those aged 14 and 15. Moreover, a 12-year-old child's level of comprehension is quite different from that of a 15-year-old because the degree of maturity must be taken into account in addition to the age factor. If we drew up a consent form with "childish" wording that would be appropriate for the 12-year-olds, the 15-year-olds might feel we were treating them paternalistically and asymmetrically. However, if we made the register of the text more complex, the 12-year-olds would not understand its aim. This led us to seek alternatives, using a single consent form approved by the committee but giving an oral explanation of the consent adapted to each age group. This adaptability was made possible by the MARVEL protocol (Silva, 2024).

3.2. MARVEL protocol, a flexible and dialogic ethical proposal

Due to the rigidity seen in ordinary research, we were drawn to come up with an ethical proposal that was truly applicable to criminological ethnographies done in cyberspace, one that would also pay special attention to fringe groups and the most vulnerable communities, like children. As we have seen, ethics focusing on regulations, which are handed down from above in the ivory towers, end up being counterproductive in the field (Van Damme, 2019). Our proposal is located down below, in the field, and is aimed at resolving the problems that arise there (Murphy & Dingwall, 2007, p. 2231). Thus, we are talking about dialogic, situational ethics (Allen, 1996), driven by negotiation between researchers and field agents. This proposal has three cornerstones:

- Situated ethics: Ethics must be adapted to the circumstances, and this principle has been advocated for more than four decades (Turner, 1984, p. 166). For this reason, stances on ethics must be taken from this position in the field (Mèlich, 2010, pp. 315–316). In other words, we are proposing putting into practice ethics that take the shape of situated knowledge (Haraway, 1988) so that in this way, we can overcome the unpredictability of the field (Conklin, 1975, p. 159; Katz, 2006, p. 500) while also helping us understand that the solutions found in some situations are not necessarily effective in others (Márquez, 2014; Silva et al., 2018). Díaz (2019, pp. 44–45) approached this stance in discussing the "ethics of skills," a situated approach focusing especially on moral values and the ethical issues that are valid in each context, aimed at finding a solution to the problems that arise. In short, this means we must accept that there are no universal assessment criteria, and we must be humble enough to understand that what might seem "correct" to an ethics committee, a moral code, or even to us may not be seen in the same light by a field agent found in a specific cultural context (Herskovits, 1976).

- Dialogic ethics: By assuming that our moral codes and ethical decisions are the valid ones, without discussing it even with the people in the field amounts to practising "moral imperialism" (Noel, 2011, p. 128). Despite the asymmetries that are always present in the field (Cerri, 2011, p. 363), it is our duty to actively listen to field agents and respond to their demands (Dietz, 2011, p. 9). It must never be a matter of imposing principles of a moral nature but rather "'ethnographying' that other moral" (Sy, 2016, p. 362), which will release us from sociocentrism and enable us to understand the foundations of the agents' demands and the proper ethical response in that regard. To focus our ethics from the field agents' perspective, we need dialogue rather than accepting preset criteria from the outset.

- Longitudinal ethics: The importance of having situated, symmetrical dialogue is not decisive if our ethical procedures continue to be deductive in nature. Ethical reflexivity cannot be set in cement at the beginning of the research by sending forms to the ethics committee or through informed consent, as we have already seen the problems that this entails. The act of reflecting on ethical matters must be constant in research both in and off the field (Estalella & Ardèvol, 2011, p. 98) because this longitudinal factor is precisely what enables us to perfect good decisions and correct our mistakes (Macfarlane, 2010, p. 25). And this is true regardless of the epistemological and analytical reflection made during the ethnographic research (Jociles, 1997, p. 98; Cerri, 2011, p. 362; Velasco & Díaz de Rada, 2013). We cannot afford to operate under the logic of "naive research"[4]

(Domingo, 2018, pp. 125–126) or the disgrace of that which is ethical[5] (Pérez, 2011), nor is it acceptable to take note of it when the research begins only to forget about it quickly after receiving approval from the ethics committee.

To achieve all this, we needed a tool that would be capable of grasping the field situation from a reflexive and analytical perspective (Díaz de Rada, 2021). That is, one that would give the researcher the option of rethinking their actions and making decisions based on gradual logic (McKenzie, 2009; Díaz de Rada, 2019), given that polarisation hinders the ability to respond to the obstacles that arise in each field of study (Sy, 2016, p. 357; Van Damme, 2019, p. 126). We managed to create such a tool, and furthermore, it is closely tied to Goals 4, 5, and 16 of the 2030 SDG, those relating to quality education, gender equality and peace, justice, and strong institutions. This tool is known as the "MARVEL protocol"[6] (Silva, 2024):

- Multivariable: The protocol could not focus on preparing a medium that measured just one research variable. It would have been much easier to link it to just one, but the fact is that there are many disparate problems we may encounter in the course of an ethnography. Therefore, with this protocol, researchers must be able to measure the variables found to be the most problematic in their fields of study.
- Analytical: The fight against attempts to ignore ethics entails analysing our practices in the field. Thus, the protocol focuses particularly on enabling researchers themselves to analyse their actions in the field.
- Reflection: Measuring variables and analysing our conduct must lead us to the next step, reflection. This is the essence of the protocol once the possible dilemmas have been identified, investigating and problematising the ethical issues we have deployed in the field. Sterile justification is not enough; we must have a space to express ourselves and defend why we did one thing or another.
- Ethical validation: This is how we manage to validate our actions in the field. In other words, the protocol allows us to defend and justify our actions so that we do not violate anyone's safety or rights in the course of the research, in addition to allowing us to use this reasoning before ethics committees.

• Longitudinal: Logically, all the above would be insufficient if it were tied to a deductive vision. That is why the protocol had to be capable of addressing the complete fieldwork. This includes the setting prior to going into the field, the field itself, and also the phase of leaving the field. Furthermore, to be consistent with the avoidance of polarisation, it must be possible to measure the variables in qualia lengths.

The protocol is implemented quite concisely in the ethnographer's work, as it takes up a single sheet of DIN A4 paper.[7] It can also be used digitally on our mobile phones or tablets. This made it very easy for us to take the protocol with us at all times, thereby replacing the ethics-bureaucracy correlation with that of ethics-reflection.

The protocol is divided into three stages corresponding to the ethical cornerstones mentioned above and the perspectives proposed by Brown (2002). First, we have the stage prior to the fieldwork, more closely related to the methodological design of the research. The second stage takes place during the fieldwork, and the third is in the analysis and dissemination period.

Each of these stages considers five variables to be measured, so the overall number of variables measured would be 15. However, on the back of the protocol, we have probe questions that could be replaced by those initially set, which can help orient us to go more in depth.[8]

These variables were measured from 1 to 4 on a Likert scale, thus avoiding the convenience of resorting to easy polarisation or always taking a central stance. In other words, it forced us to take an analytical stance and to think about gradients, reflecting on whether we were closer to yes or to no and justifying our reasons. In fact, there is a space labelled "remarks" at the end of each section for exploring these reflections more in depth, which encourages us to avoid mere numbering and explain in detail what is happening at a given time.

Finally, in the instructions to the MARVEL protocol, it clearly states that it should not be filled out all at once, establishing timelines that ensure longitudinal reflection (see Annex 2).

Thanks to this protocol, we managed to hold a symmetrical position with the field agents in which we could openly discuss ethical matters wherever possible. If this was not possible, we could establish direct communication because we were in a non-participating observation phase and simply adjusted our actions to the field norms. For example, here we can see how we discussed with the children data privacy and the communication among them during the storytelling process:

> They reflect on the different meetings where the characters are created and the people who are participating. Bryan says that at first no one posted anything and he was embarrassed. Bryan and Jimena would have preferred for everyone to be together and share ideas, so they could all contribute. Regarding Telegram, they admit that they were not very familiar with the tool and would rather have used WhatsApp [despite the fact that Telegram is more secure].
>
> (Field journal excerpt, Jorge R. Pérez)

Another example, this time referring to the non-participating observation carried out in the social media studied, can be seen in a reflection made in response to this observation:

> There she is, in front of the camera with runny mascara and a pained look. Her hair is pulled back and tears keep welling up in her eyes as she looks upward as if she were pleading for all her afflictions to end. But I can't hear her. The video has music, of course, and at the top it reads "because one day I suffered so much I almost lost my mind." It is not the first time she uploads a video about loneliness and help, but it is the first time she acknowledges serious problems, and there are followers who are still openly scolding her.
>
> (Field journal excerpt, Antonio Silva)

The reflection took place within the MARVEL protocol itself:

> The flexibility of informed consent is insufficient in some cases. We are no one's saviour and we never could have foreseen this type of situation in publicly posted content. What am I supposed to do here? Obviously, her name will be anonymised, her images pixelated or not used, but is that enough? I think the truly ethical thing to do here is to find a balance, not use images but accounts or sketches that only outline the situation. She and her safety are

what matters, so I will submit a content complaint to TikTok so that this video cannot cause her more harm.

(MARVEL protocol excerpt, Antonio Silva)

Notes

1 We are aware that following our approach, it would be more accurate to call them moral codes, but for didactic purposes and to avoid misunderstandings, we shall continue to use the common term for the time being.
2 Short audiovisual accounts of diverse problems commonly accompanied by headings that provide context. They are often used to publicly share intimate emotions (Silva et al., 2023, p. 202).
3 We need to bear in mind that from the time at which new approval is requested to the day it is received, effective days of research elapse. This means that even though we cannot conduct fieldwork until approval is granted, the days still count and the research will be impossible because of the looming deadline.
4 The kind that does not stop to think about the researcher's interests, the project objectives, the interests of the funding entity, the consequences of our actions in the field, and so forth.
5 With this, the author is referring to endeavours to ignore ethics, presuming that there are no ethical problems in our research in order to carry on in mental and administrative tranquillity.
6 See Annex 2.
7 However, it may appear somewhat longer in this book due to the publishing format.
8 This means that the protocol can also be used in other branches of sciences other than criminology.

References

Airoldi, M. (2018). Ethnography and the digital fields of social media. *International Journal of Social Research Methodology*, 21(6), 661–673.

Allen, C. (1996). What's wrong with the "golden rule"? Conundrums of conducting ethical research in cyberspace. *Information Society*, 12, 175–187.

American Anthropological Association. (2023). AAA statement on ethics: Principles of professional responsibility. https://americananthro.org/about/policies/statement-on-ethics.

Aramayo, R. (1999). El dilema kantiano entre antropología y ética. In R. Aramayo & F. Oncina (Eds.), *Ética y antropología: Un dilema kantiano* (pp. 23–42). Comares.

Bernuz, M. J., Fernández-Molina, E., Gómez, D., & De Vicente, R. (2019). La ética en la investigación criminológica. In R. Barberet, R. Bartolomé, & E. Fernández-Molina (Eds.), *Metodología de investigación en criminología* (pp. 25–45). Tirant lo Blanch.

Brown, M. (2002). *The ethical process.* Prentice Hall.

Calvey, D. (2017). *Covert research: The art, politics and ethics of undercover fieldwork.* Sage.

Cerri, C. (2011). Dilemas éticos y metodológicos en el trabajo de campo. Reflexiones de una antropóloga. *Revista de Antropología Experimental,* 11, 361–370.

Clark, T., Foster, L., Sloan, L., & Bryman, A. (2021). *Bryman's social research methods* (6th ed.). Oxford University Press.

Conklin, H. (1975). Etnografía. In J. R. Llobera (Ed.), *La antropología como ciencia* (pp. 153–166). Anagrama.

CSIC (2022). *Ética en la investigación.* Consejo Superior de Investigaciones.

Díaz, A. M. (2019). *La investigación de temas sensibles en criminología y seguridad.* Tecnos.

Díaz de Rada, Á. (2010). Bagatelas de la moralidad ordinaria. Los anclajes morales de una experiencia etnográfica. In M. Del Olmo (Ed.), *Dilemas éticos en antropología. Las entretelas del trabajo de campo etnográfico* (pp. 57–76). Trotta.

Díaz de Rada, Á. (2012, June 27). *Palabras del Profesor Ángel Díaz de Rada* [serie de entrevistas a profesionales de antropología. Éticas contemporáneas]. CanalUNED. https://canal.uned.es/video/5a6f54feb1111f6f588b4579.

Díaz de Rada, Á. (2019). *Discursos del ethnos. Una etnografía incompleta sobre procesos étnicos y etnopolíticos en el Ártico Europeo.* UNED.

Díaz de Rada, Á. (2021). Una puerta sin retorno al laberinto de las génesis. In Á. Díaz de Rada (Ed.), *Las formas del origen. Una puerta sin retorno al laberinto de las genesis* (pp. 581–630). Trotta.

Dietz, G. (2011). Hacia una etnografía doblemente reflexiva: Una propuesta desde la antropología de la interculturalidad. *AIBR, Revista de Antropología Iberoamericana,* 6(1), 3–26.

Domingo, A. (2018). *Ética de la investigación.* Herder.

Estalella, A., & Ardèvol, E. (2007). Ética de campo: Hacia una ética situada para la investigación etnográfica de internet. *FQS,* 8(3), art.2.

Estalella, A., & Ardèvol E. (2011). E-research: Desafíos y oportunidades para las ciencias sociales. *Convergencia. Revista de Ciencias Sociales,* 55, 87–111.

Fernández, M. (2010). Sujetos como objeto de estudio. In M. Del Olmo (Ed.), *Dilemas éticos en antropología. Las entretelas del trabajo de campo etnográfico* (pp. 303–314). Trotta.

Flick, U. (2015). *El diseño de investigación cualitativa.* Morata.

Gledhill, J. (2000). *El poder y sus disfraces. Perspectivas antropológicas de la política*. Bellaterra.

Gómez, E. (2008). Imagen público-privada y ética: Reflexiones desde una investigación etnográfica sobre las prácticas de fotografía digital. In E. Ardèvol, A. Estalella, & D. Domínguez (Eds.), *La mediación tecnológica en la práctica etnográfica* (pp. 183–195). Ankulegi antropologia elkartea.

Haraway, D. (1988). Situated knowledges: The science question in feminism and the privilege or partial perspective. *Feminist Studies*, 14(3), 575–599.

Heap, V., & Waters, J. (2019). *Mixed methods in criminology*. Routledge.

Herskovits, M. (1976). *El hombre y sus obras*. Fondo de Cultura Económica.

Jociles, M. I. (1997). Nigel Barley y la investigación etnográfica. *Política y Sociedad*, 24, 97–120.

Kant, E. (2005). *La metafísica de las costumbres*. Tecnos.

Kant, E. (2013). *Crítica de la razón pura*. Taurus.

Katz, J. (2006). Ethical escape routes for underground ethnographers. *American Ethnologist*, 33(4), 499–506.

Latour, B. (2007). *Nunca fuimos modernos. Ensayo de antropología simétrica*. Siglo XXI.

Lederman, R. (2006). The perils of working at home: IRB "mission creep" as context for an ethnography of disciplinary knowledges. *American Ethnologist*, 33, 482–491.

Lehner-Mear, R. (2019). Negotiating the ethics of netnography: Developing an ethical approach to an online study of mother perspectives. *International Journal of Social Research Methodology*, 23(2), 123–137. https://doi.org/10.1080/13645579.2019.1634879.

Macfarlane, B. (2010). Values and virtues in qualitative research. In M. Saven-Baden & C. Howell (Eds.), *In new approach to qualitative research: Wisdom an uncertainty* (pp. 18–27). Routledge.

Márquez, I. (2014). Ética de la investigación etnográfica en los cibermundos. *Anthropologica*, 32(33), 111–135.

McKenzie, J. (2009). "You don't know how lucky you are to be here!": Reflections on covert practices in an overt participant observation study. *Sociological Research Online*, 14(2). doi:10.5153/sro.1925.

Mèlich, J. C. (2010). Poética de lo íntimo (sobre ética y antropología). *Ars Brevis*, 16, 314–331.

Muñoz, R., & Salinas, C. (2018). La crisis de la autoridad del etnografiado. Metodologías encubiertas e investigación en derechos humanos y población vulnerable: Dos estudios de caso en México. *Estudios de Género de El Colegio de México*, 4(19), 1–34.

Murphy, E., & Dingwall, R. (2007). Informed consent, anticipatory regulation and ethnographic practice. *Social Science & Medicine*, 65(11), 2223–2234.

Noel, G. (2011). Algunos dilemas éticos del trabajo antropológico con actores implicados en actividades delictivas. *Ankulegi. Revista de Antropología Social*, 15, 127–137.

Ojeda de López, J., Quintero, J., & Machado, I. (2007). La ética en la investigación. *TeloS*, 9(2), 345–357.

Pérez, B. (2011). "Y esto, a mí, ¿para qué me sirve, señorita?" Implicaciones éticas y políticas de la etnografía en contextos de violencia, pobreza y desigualdad. *Ankulegi*, 15, 103–114.

Real Academia de la Lengua Española. (2024). *Diccionario*. Real Academia Española. https://www.rae.es.

Schrag, Z. (2010). *Ethical imperialism: Institutional review boards and the social sciences, 1965–2009*. Johns Hopkins University Press.

Silva, A. (2019). Etnografía [des]encubierta. Una mirada a la práctica etnográfica encubierta del Ultra Realismo criminológico [unpublished master's thesis]. UNED.

Silva, A. (2024). Dando forma a las sombras. Comprendiendo la construcción del conocimiento y el dispositivo encubierto en las etnografías del Ultra-Realismo [doctoral dissertation, UNED]. http://e-spacio.uned.es/fez/view/tesisuned:ED-Pg-DivSubSoc-Asilva

Silva, A., Pérez, J. R., & Briggs, D. (2018). El escuadrón suicida de la criminología. Innovación etnográfica en contextos de ocio nocturno. Casos Magaluf y "raves." *Archivos de Criminología, Seguridad Privada y Criminalística*, 21, 109–134.

Stark, L. (2012). *Behind closed doors: IRBs and the making of ethical research*. University of Chicago Press.

Steenhout, I. (2013). Facing resistance to research results. In K. Beyens, J. Christiaens, B. Claes, S. De Ridder, H. Tournel, & H. Tubex (Eds.), *The pains of doing criminological research* (pp. 181–193). Vubpress.

Sy, A. (2016). Ética en el trabajo de campo: Una reflexión desde la experiencia etnográfica. *Revista de Antropología Experimental*, 16, 353–363.

Turner, S. (1984). *La explicación sociológica como traducción*. Fondo de Cultura Económica.

Van Damme, E. (2019). When overt research feels covert: Researching women and gangs in a context of silence and fear. *Journal of Extreme Anthropology*, 3(1). https://doi.org/10.5617/jea.6696.

Velasco, H., & Díaz de Rada, Á. (2013). *La lógica de la investigación etnográfica: Un modelo de trabajo para etnógrafos de la escuela*. Trotta.

4 Uploading stories
Weaving digital ethnography

Now that we have given a brief introduction of the studies, the problems in the academic setting, and the proper ethical approach to ethnographic research on young people, the time has come to discuss the method used: ethnography.

4.1. Ethnography and its challenges

At GCIPS, we feel that more than an isolated or confined method, ethnography is the research logic followed in the field of study (Velasco & Díaz de Rada, 2013, p. 10). In other words, ethnography, in our opinion, is based on the conception of research itself, or how we attain empirical materials, how we process them, how we create written texts based on the above, and so forth. This is what renders so flexible the methodological dynamics in play during the research.

However, given that in academia we usually prefer fixed definitions, we agree with Hammersley and Atkinson's (1994, p. 15) proposal. They define ethnography as the method or set of methods whereby an ethnographer openly or covertly participates in everyday settings for a period of time. That time spent in the field is used to observe the actions performed, to listen carefully to what is said, and to ask whenever necessary. This methodological position enables the ethnographer to compile sufficient empirical materials to fulfil the research aims.

Taking this definition as the basis, ethnographers may assume diverse observation roles, although none of them can be deemed as isolated or fixed, given that they may vary during the course of a

DOI: 10.4324/9781003399315-4

research project. In this regard, the traditional categorisation described by Gold (1958, cited in Angrosino, 2012, pp. 80–81) is paradigmatic.

- Complete observer, also described in scientific literature as non-participant observation (Riba, 2013): This role is detached from the field agents, and there is no intention to interact with them but to go unobserved and record as much data as possible. It is the role most closely linked to the natural sciences and, as such, claims to be the most "objective."
- Observer as participant: In this role, the researcher does interact with the field agents and is identified as such. In this case, the observations are usually brief and geared more toward compiling sufficient empirical material to conduct interviews at a later stage.
- Participant as observer: This would be the next step in the logic of interaction with the field agents. The researcher is introduced as such, spends more time with the agents, and moral anchors begin to emerge.[1]
- Complete participant: This is when the ethnographer begins to identify strongly with the field agents and with the setting itself. In this role, it is not uncommon for the researcher to "go native," focusing more on matters that drive the every-day life of the social group studied than on the research being conducted.

Regardless of the profile used, we must always bear in mind the pillars of description, translation, and interpretation in ethnography. Ethnographic description requires density (Geertz, 1973). In other words, it is not about making a quick sketch of the field actions but studying the structures of meaning we generally tend to ignore and making descriptions and interpretations with the greatest possible degree of detail. In turn, when we talk about translating, we are not drawing a parallel to linguistic translation but rather making a direct reference to the principles of Evans-Pritchard (1973): that is, we need to understand the studied phenomenon from the perspective of how it is conceived by the field agents in order to subsequently translate it into valid interpretable concepts for the scientific or other communities. Finally, the aim of the interpretation work is to draw lines between the thick description and the culture in which the phenomenon takes place rather than analysing it in an ethnocentric way.

4.2. Unique features of digital ethnography and our stance in this regard

Up to now, we have given a brief definition of our understanding of ethnography at GCIPS. However, every method or set of methods evolves over time. Thus, with the emergence of the internet and the conception of the cyborg (Haraway, 1990), the need for conceptualisations inherent to cyberspace began to arise in the field. Hine (2000, 2015) recognised this in the change of position between her works, but we identify much more with the approach or proposal offered by Pink et al. (2016) because it creates a friendly dialogue with the concept of "research logic followed in the field" (Velasco & Díaz de Rada, 2013) referred to above. Pink et al. (2016) consider digital ethnography to be a gradual or adaptive process based on the following premises:

- Multiplicity: Digital ethnography cannot be seen as a laboratory protocol. There is no step one, followed by a second step, and completed by a third. Sometimes the research is guided by theories established in the theoretical framework, while other times it is driven by the participants' needs or the requirements of the funding entities. In short, we must view it as adaptive ethnography.
- Non-digital-centricness: Technology affects us, and we affect it, as Latour (2008) said, or we have become technology directly, according to Haraway (1990). Based on these premises, we must understand that digital ethnography is not based only on a device or on its use but on an entire relational setting.
- Openness: Digital ethnography is flexible, hybrid, dialogic, and cross-disciplinary. It cannot be conceived as something limited or closed.
- Reflexivity: The way in which knowledge is generated from the empirical material collected becomes especially interesting in this type of ethnography. Cyberspace is immense, and drawing superficial borders to make it easier to construct intersubjective

frameworks would be sterile. For this reason, the ethnographer has more work to do in this regard.

- Unorthodox: Digital ethnography forces us to move beyond the traditional methods of dissemination or conveying results (papers and books)[2] in an effort to have a greater community impact by using formats such as websites, social media, blogs,[3] and so forth.

To sum up, we could describe digital ethnography as a qualitative research technique that focuses on understanding the dynamics found within a field of digital study, its composition and structure, the relationships between its agents, and so forth in order to then "translate" (Turner, 1984) these findings to the academic community and/or society in general.

4.2.1. Reflections on covert practices in digital spaces

We would like to go back to the definition of ethnography by Hammersley and Atkinson (1994), specifically the part that refers to covert practices. The reason for this is mainly because this detail is even easier to implement in a digital setting. Covert ethnographic research could be defined as that which is conducted without the knowledge of the field agents or where there is an absence of informed consent (O'Reilly, 2008, p. 44). In other words, ethnography in which the researcher decides not to reveal his/her/their identity to the agents (Holloway, 1997, p. 39) and poses as a member of the community while conducting social experiments (Bloor & Ward, 2006, p. 43).

This practice has been frowned upon, linked to malpractice, ethical violations, and viewed as a uniformly conducted practice, yet this could not be further from the truth (Silva, 2019). Precisely because of the disparate ways of conceptualising and conducting it, we support the thesis that we must view it either as a cultural artifact (Isava, 2009, p. 144) or an epistemic one[4] (Vega, 2005), or as a device[5] (Agamben, 2015).

Expressed like this, perhaps our stance is a bit difficult to comprehend. We shall use a quote from Geertz (1973) to give it a sturdier support:

> Our ideas, our values, our acts, even our emotions, are, like our nervous system itself, cultural products—products manufactured, indeed, out of tendencies, capacities, and dispositions

with which we were born, but manufactured nonetheless. Chartres is made of stone and glass. But it is not just stone and glass; it is a cathedral, and not only a cathedral, but a particular cathedral built at a particular time by certain members of a particular society. To understand what it means, to perceive it for what it is, you need to know rather more than the generic properties of stone and glass and rather more than what is common to all cathedrals. You need to understand also—and, in my opinion, most critically—the specific concepts of the relations among God, man, and architecture that, since they have governed its creation, it consequently embodies. It is no different with men: they, too, every last one of them, are cultural artifacts.

(p. 56)

Thus, covert practice must be accepted as an artifact impregnated with a signifying width[6] (Isava, 2009, p. 440). Of course, one artifact or another may differ in appearance, but what defines them as such is that they were conceived through human ingenuity (Martos & Martos, 2014, p. 120). Therefore, they may be intangible constructs (Holland & Cole, 1995), as is the case with covert practices.

We cannot view covert ethnographic practices as a uniform whole but rather as a cultural artifact or a device that may or may not be used ethically, depending on the subject, just like any other research method. In fact, what we should ask ourselves here is whether there are any purely open research methods or even whether it is possible to be strictly open in the digital field (Silva, 2024). At any rate, we will discuss these matters further at the end of the chapter.

4.2.2. The use of digital ethnography in our projects

We hope that by now the reader has some idea about our epistemological and methodological stance. Therefore, now is the time to briefly describe the field of study and its agents.

The ethnographic fieldwork in CONFIDOMINA2.NET[7] took place in the "metafield" (Airoldi, 2018) composed of Instagram, TikTok, and Twitch. On these platforms, a detailed study was conducted of 15 minors and all the content they produced, a total of more than 10,000 videos:[8]

Table 4.1 Composition of the CONFIDOMINA2.NET sample

Subject	Gender	Current age	Starting age	Followers (millions)	Videos
1	F	16	12	2.3	1546
2	F	18	14	9.4	441
3	F	18	13	4.1	4032
4	F	18	12	7.7	3340
5	F	17	14	2.1	921
6	M	18	17	1.3	833
7	M	14	14	2.2	2079
8	M	17	17	4.8	381
9	M	15	13	4.8	1784
10	M	14	13	1.1	1264

Source: Compiled by authors. Madrid, 2023.

The role of complete observer was used for the ethnography in this project. That is, we merely studied the actions performed by the children without coming into direct contact with them. The intention was to foster care in research ethics to respect minors' rights, to which end we implemented the MARVEL protocol (Silva, 2024) to ensure their safety, operating according to the rules allowed in the field of study.

It is important, however, to briefly describe the context in which the study was conducted. On 14 March 2020, Spain's prime minister, Pedro Sánchez, declared a state of emergency as a result of the health crisis caused by COVID-19.[9] Measures were imposed in relation to the freedom of movement, teaching activities were suspended, and establishments open to the public were closed. Therefore, universities and schools began online schooling, and families were forced to spend time working and studying at home, wherever possible, with their computers. Subsequently, according to the Constitutional Court (Tribunal Constitucional, 2021), this royal decree was declared partially unconstitutional as regards the lockdown and the restrictions on freedom of movement.

Such was the case that the sample studied showed an increase in TikTok posts during or immediately after the lockdown. Many of them created their accounts right at that time. As there were few other options for socialising, the early months of the lockdown witnessed a prolific amount of content creation, without bearing in mind the repercussions that this all had in terms of mental, physical, and emotional health. According to the chronicle made during the ethnography, we see that

> Leto began by posting 70–80 videos per month on average, then dropping to around 40, Vladimir began by posting 386 videos per month and then dropping to some 90–100, Duncan reached 84 a month before coming to an average of 15 and Stilgar from around 120 to 20. Nearly all the girls were more prolific than the boys. However, it is true that nearly all of them had begun years earlier on this platform or even from its predecessor platform (musica.ly). At any rate, Lucia went from posting some 40–50 videos per month to around 90–110, Chani went from about 90–100 to 250–290 a month.
>
> (Ethnographic note on frequency, field journal, Antonio Silva)

Not only is it interesting in this regard to contemplate the number of posts but also the minors' ability to believe themselves invulnerable to the health rules and recommendations during lockdown. As an example:

- Paul not only travelled constantly during lockdown, but he even held parties. Furthermore, he had his father's permission to do so.
- Leto stopped wearing a mask when he was in contact with numerous people. This led him to get COVID-19.
- Alia went so far as to travel to Latin America during regional lockdown periods.
- Alia, Jessica, and other friends appear in a video of another famous influencer cheering the pandemic while none of them were wearing a mask.
- Vladimir, Jessica, and Irulan, among others, defended themselves from accusations about travelling or not wearing masks. The basis of their reasoning was that the public could only see what they chose to display, not what actually took place behind the camera.

4.3. Some relevant findings

We would like to highlight some of the findings we consider to be important here, not so much in terms of the findings themselves but because of the connection between the methodology developed in our ethnography and the type of empirical materials it afforded us on an analytical level. Thus, rather than discussing these findings in detail, our aim is to offer a general overview that enables the reader to trace possible means of access to certain research phenomena from a methodological stance similar to ours.

4.3.1. *Fetishisation of adulthood and democratisation of celebrity*

If one thing is present in social media, it is digital hyperstimulation (Gértrudix, Borges, & García, 2017). Myriads of posts with diverse, explicit content appear as objects of desire in an economic environment dominated by consumption. That yearning is polymorphic. It sometimes emerges as a desire for a public image or for popularity, appearance, inclusion in peer groups, and so forth. This matter can end up affecting children negatively:

> And so it is when I suddenly see a 15-year-old boy put the following text in his video: "The best thing that could happen to us would be to go back to being children, because scraped knees definitely hurt less than broken hearts." They've already lived it all, for practical purposes they live an adult life. At least in front of the camera. They work, travel, have cars, spend summers in mansions, have significant amounts of money, fall in and out of love, have sex, drink alcohol and take drugs, have an incomparable social status. What is left for them to experience at this age?
>
> (Field journal excerpt, Antonio Silva)

Ethnographic access to this type of content allows us to thoroughly evaluate the period in which young people are transformed, whether they act as influencers or as followers that let themselves be influenced. We do not interfere in their lives or establish contact with them; we act according to the rules allowed in the field—we are mere observers in a "public" field. However, one might argue that what is conveyed over these social media is nothing more than a "simulation" (Baudrillard, 1978). This is where the ethnographer's analytical capacity comes into full play to comprehend the field without being swept away by "allegory" (Clifford, 1986). Our task is to understand and translate (Benjamin, 2017), and we must do so according to the experiences of our agents, not constructing the field ourselves. Subsequently, we can progress analytically based on that empirical material by taking appropriate epistemological stances; in this case, for example, Latour's (2008) actor-network perspective would be highly useful.

4.3.2. Pornography of pain

Elsewhere, we have discussed the selfie culture and the problems it generated (Pérez, 2017). Now, a few years later (with all that this implies in technological settings), we have seen how it has evolved toward what we have termed the "pornography of pain." As cyborgs (Haraway, 1990), we are not just permeable to the digital world; we are actually part of it. In the case of boys and girls, this matter becomes even more predominant for diverse reasons (less self-control, more free time, the inclusion of technology with greater force in everyday life, neuroplasticity, etc.). This occurs to such an extent that the cyborg reaches its ultimate expression, and young people sometimes no longer feel able to distinguish between the online world and the physical one, between fiction and reality. In a sense "The Real" (Lacan, 2013) has been taken hostage.

Within this setting, contents emerge in which young people can be seen experiencing tragic scenes relating to a wide range of what they deem to be their everyday problems. Somehow, they choose one of these problems and depict it for the social media, adapting it to the format on each platform.[10] This type of content is usually classified under the acronym POV (point of view) and is launched as a wager for connection to the rest of the community. Therefore, they include issues such as pain, insecurity, depression, addiction, and more and serve as a catalyst for gaining followers or loyalty.

The permeability of the digital world in young people's lives, and even the fusion of the two realms for many of them, prompts some of them to be unable to distinguish reality from fiction. This is particularly concerning when it comes to those histrionic contents in which young people depict themselves playing out tragic stories about diverse problems, accompanied by music with simple, reductionist lyrics they find appropriate, usually with headings to offer some context. Some youths publicly share intimate emotions indiscriminately this way, converting pain and insecurity into a fetish aimed at garnering the public's attention (Silva et al., 2023). It could be said that this arises from a sort of confusion between performance and experience, which ultimately leads to another confusion – namely, whether they are publicly conveying something private or if they are able to discern between what is public and what is private.

Precisely by following ethnographic research logic, we were able to observe that the community also reacted to these ups and downs in diverse ways, ranging from support to utterly scathing criticism. This created an even more toxic environment in which the confusion as to whether the content was being posted by a real or feigned boy or girl was compounded by the verbal violence of the public. If the experience proved to be true, what it ultimately unleashed was victimisation of several kinds and a normalisation of violence:

> [X] is angry because she says that TikTok has gone from being a democratic platform where everyone did whatever they wanted and nobody criticised anything to a space for hate that is used to attack others for any reason. She insists that if the hate is aimed at her, it doesn't matter because she has strong self-esteem. But if it is against her friends, relatives or people who have nothing to do with it, this is not acceptable.
>
> (Field journal excerpt, Antonio Silva)

In fact, by following a logic that is "non-digital-centricness" (Pink et al., 2016) throughout our ethnographic process, we were able to confirm that many of the cases presumed to be theatrical under the "POV" label proved to be actual vulnerabilities in the end:

> There she is, in front of the camera with runny mascara and a pained look. Her hair is pulled back and tears keep welling up in her eyes as she looks upward as if she were pleading for all her afflictions to end. But I can't hear her. The video has music,

of course, and at the top it reads "because one day I suffered so much I almost lost my mind." It is not the first time she uploads a video about loneliness and help, but it is the first time she acknowledges serious problems, and there are followers who are still openly scolding her.

(Field journal excerpt, Antonio Silva)

Therefore, our findings seemed to indicate that the type of digital production and the way of consuming within this setting ultimately increased the likelihood of boys and girls experiencing periods of profound confusion, distortions, and cognitive dissonance. All of these issues are difficult to access "from down below" unless a methodology similar to ours is implemented.

4.3.3. Social harm in young people

Another important avenue that the ethnography allowed us to explore was the concept of social harm. Sometimes we focused solely on studying, from a criminological viewpoint, phenomena classified as crimes or deviation. However, there are countless types of conduct that are not defined in laws or provisions governing the community that do indeed cause significant harm in the community (Hillyard & Tombs, 2004; Hall, 2012; Yar, 2012; Pemberton, 2016; Kotzé, 2018; Raymen, 2019). Given that the theoretical framework on social harm is precarious and fragmented (Raymen, 2019), a brief summary is offered here for context:

Table 4.2 Classification of social harm

Hillyard & Tombs (2004)	Pemberton (2016)	Hall & Winlow (2015)
Physical harm	Physical or mental health harms	Negative motivation to harm
Financial and economic harm	Autonomy harms	Positive motivation to harm (special liberty)
Emotional and psychological harm	Relational harms (exclusion and misrecognition)	
Threats to cultural safety		

Source: Compiled by Cordero et al. (2022, p. 5). Valencia, 2023.

As we can see, there is no single definition of social harm. And this is the case precisely because it would be doomed to failure otherwise. The concept of social harm must adapt to new phenomena (Raymen, 2019, p. 152) that could arise not only in the economic sphere (Hall, 2012, p. 16) but also in interpersonal environments (Yar, 2012, p. 58). Ultimately, what matters is that if they are seen as harm entailing a "social mediation" (Pemberton, 2016, pp. 25–26), that would make it possible to prevent or manage them.

The digital ethnography was extremely useful in pinpointing phenomena that could be classified as social harm to boys and girls. However, rather than implementing a procedure based on deductive logical inference (Castañares, 1994) to detect them, we used abductive reasoning (Peirce, 2012; Díaz de Rada, 2021) to understand what was really happening in the field. We began by finding a considerable compendium of empirical material that evidenced problems or risks related to the youths' mental health. We are referring to insecurities, anxiety, addiction, false empowerment, fatphobia, eating disorders, and so forth:

> The most significant cases of insecurity, anxiety and addiction are seen in Irulan and Chani. The path is like an exceedingly cruel emotional roller coaster. First, they suffer for one reason or another; then, they tell the community about how devastated they are, and the more they talk about it, the more merciless the community is with them.
>
> (Field journal excerpt, Antonio Silva)

We needed to discern where this tendency came from, beyond the usual correlates put forward in scientific literature (Echeburúa & De Corral, 2010; Portillo et al., 2021; Lozano-Muñoz et al., 2022; López et al., 2023). In other words, we wanted to find out whether there was a distinguishing factor in this field that fostered this kind of conduct. The power of the algorithm came to our aid here. We do not mean the algorithm defined as "a finite, abstract, effective compound control structure given imperatively that meets a determined purpose under certain preconditions" (Hill, 2016, p. 47) but rather the algorithm following the notion of social imagination (Cabrera, 2021, pp. 125–145): that is, in the capacity to have an impact on sociocultural work.

As researchers, we could not avoid the control that the algorithm exerted over us in our fieldwork. Therefore, from a coherent analytical position, what we did was to let ourselves be led by it, just like any other agent in the field, but with a critical gaze not often used in our daily lives in this type of digital environment. As such, we were able to discern where it tends to lead young people and why it does so. Here, we might mention brand advertising that encourages the purchase of cosmetics or clothing, betting, food, and so forth, but what matters most is that we found that the influence that the algorithm of these networks could have on minors represents a very powerful predictor of social harm.

One example is their capacity to influence young people so that they end up believing that the utopic lives of influencers are actually possible. The algorithm is able to achieve that degree of influence based on repetition of the content generated by those influencers. Another clear example is related to metafields (Airoldi, 2018). In other words, the different digital environments (social media, applications, etc.) are linked to each other in numerous ways, and companies have harnessed this opportunity by owning several applications or social media platforms[11] in order to link and share linguistic codes that emphasise all of this.

Therefore, we believe that an ethnographic logic based on metafields is essential for criminological studies of social harm in areas like the ones discussed here. Otherwise, detecting and fully understanding the ultimate victimisation situations would be much more complex and ineffective.

4.4. Lessons learned

Despite the fact that we already mentioned in the previous section the benefits that ethnography has to offer in terms of access to certain phenomena, we wish to reflect briefly on more purely methodological considerations that could be of interest to the reader when it comes to current or future research. In other words, we want to share the lessons we learned for you to perform, improve on, critique, or adapt them to your research. We can summarise them in three lessons. One is related to covert practices in ethnographic work, another focuses more on the concept of "lurking," and the last has to do with cross-cutting benefits in terms of methodology.

4.4.1. Advantages/disadvantages of covert practices

At the beginning of the chapter, we gave an overview of the covert artifact or device but did not go into detail with respect to the advantages and obstacles that could arise in practice. Even though there are probably no purely open research methods (Silva, 2024) and the digital environment itself affords a structure that often renders it impossible to be open due to the cultural norms of each metafield (Airoldi, 2018), the covert device or artifact continues to be penalised in general.

The assumption of covert practices is quickly associated with malpractice by ethics committees. However, this is inconsistent from the outset given that the supposed remedy for everything, informed consent, is nothing more than another means of concealment: anonymity is just another level on the scale of concealment. In fact, if we declare that we plan to perform non-participant or naturalist observation (Silva, 2020), our research projects are likely to be approved because these categories stem from the biomedical sciences and are not questioned. It would appear that no one has stopped to think that precisely this type of observation makes the utmost use of the covert device or artifact.

In sum, although we were aware that an ethnography in which covert practices were implemented would offer a better understanding of the phenomenon and that we would act ethically at all times, the fact is that declaring our methodology in such terms was paramount to "project denied." With this, we are not encouraging anyone to use certain terms and then to act differently based on a naive research logic (Domingo, 2018). What we are addressing is a methodological problem that we must solve as soon as possible through dialogue with our ethics committees.

Furthermore, adopting a covert device or artifact in certain parts of our research may also afford benefits. The most obvious would be access to phenomena that are off-limits because they take place in closed locations. Because they cannot be seen, these phenomena cannot be studied, and if they are not studied, they do not exist for the community and cannot be prevented or managed. As social scientists, we cannot lay the foundations on which victimisation and opacity are built, for our work consists in doing the exact opposite.

In addition, the covert device or artifact also helps us to avoid much of the social desirability bias or altering the dynamics in the field. We must bear in mind that we are adult researchers and, by definition, we have an absolutely asymmetrical position in relation to the young people. Not only would they not trust us (and especially not in a digital environment), but they would always try to respond in the way they thought they should respond to an adult. In this way, the spontaneity of the environment and the actions performed there is lost. This may not always be the case, but it is highly likely to occur. However, a responsibly implemented covert device or artifact makes it possible to enter and leave the field without rendering any potentially destabilising changes while also gaining an understanding of the dynamics under the usual conditions.

As a final advantage, although some may initially object, we will mention that a covert device or artifact can (and should) make both the researcher and the research subject feel more secure. If the minors know that some adults called "researchers" or "criminologists" are asking them questions about what they do in their social media, in all likelihood they will feel under pressure, anxious, harassed, or victimised. Is it necessary to base our actions on this logic? Sometimes, depending on the phenomenon studied, the nearest thing to an open position will be most appropriate. Other times, when the conduct has ties to crime, studying the phenomenon under a covert device or artifact will provide greater confidentiality for the field agents while also keeping us safer behind an anonymous account. This matter also has an impact on the subsequent production or spread of empirical materials in that it enables us to draw a link to help locate the field agents.

4.4.2. Lurker

Within a gradual conception of covert practices, there is one that is generally referred to by the name of "lurker." In an early text, Canetti (2012) described this position in the field in an extremely elegant manner:

> Secrecy lies at the very core of power. The act of lying in wait for prey is essentially secret. Hiding, or taking on the colour of its surroundings and betraying itself by no movement, the

lurking creature disappears entirely, covering itself with secrecy as with a second skin. This state, which can last for a long time, is characterised by a peculiar blend of patience and impatience and the longer it lasts, the fiercer becomes the anticipation of the moment of success. But in order to achieve success in the end the watcher must be capable of endless patience. If this breaks a moment too soon everything will have been in vain and, weighed down with disappointment, he must start again from the beginning.

(p. 67)

In short, this position is quite similar to the role of non-participant observer mentioned above. The exception is that here the ethnographer does not remain static – quite the opposite. Adopting this position was highly useful in order to efficiently address the ethical requirements, on the one hand, and, on the other hand, to perform a thorough observation in a setting in which the boundaries between public and private are unclear, avoiding as much as possible any impact of any kind on the boys and girls.

Sometimes it could be argued that, as this position gives the ethnographer the ability to "see through other men, but does not allow them to see through them" (Canetti, 2012, p. 67), this is an example of domination and a violation of rights. There is no doubt that this could be the case in the event of malpractice. However, in our case, our intention was never to create asymmetry or domination, although asymmetry is an underlying element of any method, whether it is conducted covertly or openly.[12]

At any rate, in the metafields that we focused on during our research with young people, we operated as if we were another field agent. That means viewing the content they generated or reading the chat comments. We never even shared a post or used the "like" button. Furthermore, our account showed that we were researchers at work. However, perhaps because so many users view their contents or maybe because someone thought the fact that we were researchers was a joke, the truth is that there were never any conflicts during the fieldwork. We believe it was precisely because the most common practice in these settings is exactly that: viewing content and moving on.[13]

4.4.3. Dichotomous interactions

The final item we wish to draw attention to is the benefit afforded by a properly thick description (Geertz, 1973) throughout our digital ethnographies. We are aware, as indeed we mentioned at the beginning, that digital ethnography is not merely applying traditional ethnographic techniques to the digital environment. It would be relatively easy to believe that a thick description (Geertz, 1973) would not be so important in a sporadic, malleable environment like cyberspace. Nothing could be further from the truth.

This technique gives us not only a much better understanding of our field, its inhabitants, and the actions they perform in relation to our research goals. What happens is that in that learning and translation process, those goals are exceeded and certain empirical materials begin to emerge before us that help us continue moving forward and to hone our methodological strategies.

Such was the case during our research that we were able to much better comprehend the youths' actions and reactions in the social media. In other words, we gained an understanding of the interface that has been erected between humans and technology, which made us more sensitive to the codes that have been set up in the social media and the collective and individual meanings that the children assigned to them. Pink et al. (2016) spoke of this when they mentioned "socialities" as a new way of conceptualising and understanding the experiences in these digital environments. In short, what they suggested was that it was necessary to understand this new way of assigning meanings, and we could not agree more. By thoroughly understanding these actions, we were able to develop a micro-survey method based on the dichotomous interactions often used by the young people. Thus, we verified afterwards that by using metafield logic, appropriate language, an audiovisual context, and a rapid dichotomous response, the rate of response to our surveys increased. We even found that using the logic of intermittency, the outcome was better yet if we asked the questions in different waves instead of grouping them in a single post.

Notes

1 We are referring to the ethnographer's moral ties to the people in the field (Díaz de Rada, 2010, p. 58).

2 It would be interesting to ask ourselves right now, what are we doing writing a book about this if we are following these principles? Basically, this book is not about research outcomes but rather of a methodological nature. In such cases, this is usually the required format because sharing is customary within academia, and therefore, this is the format that will be most useful to researchers. That said, we have indeed been posting the results in formats such as blogs and social media.

3 Such as the group's blog, Investigación Criminológica – Blog del Grupo de Conocimiento-Investigación en Problemáticas Sociales (UE) (hypoth eses.org).

4 Vega (2005, p. 23) would say that a significant portion of human actions are aimed at modifying the structure of the information that surrounds us to assimilate it better. So-called epistemic artefacts are classified within this set of actions aimed at improving efficiency in the extraction of information.

5 It is "literally anything that in some way has the capacity to capture, orient, determine, intercept, model, control, or secure the gestures, behaviours, opinions, or discourses of living beings" (Agamben, 2015, p. 23). For further information, see Silva (2024, pp. 189–190).

6 That is, a width such that it is possible to move beyond the conventional conception of the mere artifact, which is not restricted to one purpose or to psychoanalytical or economic aspects but transcends the symbolic (Isava, 2009, p. 448).

7 The work done in A.I.DRIANA will be discussed in the next chapter due to its uniqueness.

8 This figure does not include all the comments analysed of each post, photographs, or the more secondary study of other profiles.

9 Through Royal Decree 463/2020 of 14 March, whereby a state of emergency is declared for the management of the health crisis situation caused by COVID-19.

10 On TikTok, for example, they adjust it for timing, adding music, headings for context, and so forth.

11 Amazon with Twitch or Facebook with Instagram and WhatsApp are good examples.

12 We are referring here to the fact that in the end, as researchers, we will always have a privileged position over field agents. We have advantages from the outset, not only relating to ethnicity, social position, and so on but also relating to the fact that we are there in an analytical capacity equipped with theoretical knowledge before going into the field.

13 Which is another definition of "lurker," acting as an "onlooker."

References

Agamben, G. (2015). *¿Qué es un dispositivo?*Anagrama.

Airoldi, M. (2018). Ethnography and the digital fields of social media. *International Journal of Social Research Methodology*, 21(6), 661–673.

Angrosino, M. (2012). *Etnografía y observación participante en investigación cualitativa*. Morata.

Baudrillard, J. (1978). *Cultura y simulacro*. Kairós.

Benjamin, W. (2017). *La tarea del traductor*. Sequitur.

Bloor, M., & Ward, F. (2006). *Keywords in qualitative methods: A vocabulary of research concepts*. Sage.

Cabrera, D. H. (2021). El algoritmo como imaginario social. *ZER*, 26(50), 125–145.

Canetti, E. (2012). Secreto y poder. *Revista Occidente*, 374–375, 67–75.

Castañares, W. (1994). *De la interpretación a la lectura*. Iberoediciones.

Clifford, J. (1986). On ethnographic allegory. In J. Clifford & G. Marcus (Eds.), *Writing culture: The poetics and politics of ethnography*. University of California Press.

Cordero, R., Silva, A., & Pérez, J. R. (2022). The invisible suffering of young people during the COVID-19 pandemic in Spain and the collateral impact of social harm. *Social Sciences*, 11(8), 335. doi:10.3390/socsci11080335.

Cordero, R., Silva, A., Pérez, J. R., & Gómez, F. (2021). *El challenge based research (CBR) como reto pedagógico. La investigación en criminología llevada a la docencia*. McGraw Hill.

Díaz de Rada, Á. (2010). Bagatelas de la moralidad ordinaria. Los anclajes morales de una experiencia etnográfica. In M. Del Olmo (Ed.), *Dilemas éticos en antropología. Las entretelas del trabajo de campo etnográfico* (pp. 57–76). Trotta.

Díaz de Rada, Á. (2021). Una puerta sin retorno al laberinto de las génesis. In Á. Díaz de Rada (Ed.), *Las formas del origen. Una puerta sin retorno al laberinto de las génesis* (pp. 581–630). Trotta.

Domingo, A. (2018). *Ética de la investigación*. Herder.

Echeburúa, E., & De Corral, P. (2010). Adicción a las nuevas tecnologías y a las redes sociales en jóvenes un nuevo reto. *Adicciones*, 22(2), 91–95.

Evans-Pritchard, E. (1973). *Las teorías de la religión primitiva*. Siglo XXI Editores.

Geertz, C. (1973). *The interpretation of cultures*. Basic Books.

Gértrudix, M., Borges, E., & García, F. (2017). Redes sociales y jóvenes en la era algorítmica. *TELOS*, 107, 62–70.

Gold, R. L. (1958). Roles in sociological field observations. *Social Forces*, 36, 217–223.

Hall, S. (2012). Consumer culture and the meaning of the urban riots in England. In S. Hall & S. Winlow (Eds.), *New directions in criminological theory* (pp. 145–164). Routledge.

Hall, S., & Winlow, S. (2015). *Revitalizing criminological theory: Towards a new ultra-realism*. Routledge.

Hammersley, M., & Atkinson, P. (1994). *Etnografía: Métodos de investigación*. Paidós Ibérica.

Haraway, D. (1990). *Simians, cyborgs, and women: The reinvention of nature*. Routledge. https://doi.org/10.4324/9780203873106.

Hill, R. (2016). What an algorithm is? *Philosophy and Technology*, 29, 35–59.

Hillyard, P., & Tombs, S. (2004). *Beyond criminology: Taking harm seriously*. Pluto Press.

Hine, C. (2000). *Virtual ethnography*. Sage.

Hine, C. (2015). *Ethnography for the internet: Embedded, embodied and everyday*. Bloomsbury.

Holland, D., & Cole, M. (1995). Between discourse and schema: Reformulating a cultural-historical approach to culture and mind. *Anthropology and Education Quarterly*, 26(4), 475–490. doi:10.1525/aeq.1995.26.4.05x1065y.

Holloway, I. (1997). *Basic concepts for qualitative research*. Wiley-Blackwell.

Isava, L. M. (2009). Breve introducción a los artefactos culturales. *Estudios*, 17(34), 439–452.

Kotzé, J. (2018). Criminology or zemiology? Yes, please! On the refusal of choice between false alternatives. In A. Boukli & J. Kotzé (Eds.), *Zemiology: Critical criminological perspectives* (pp. 85–106). Palgrave Macmillan.

Lacan, J. (2013). *Escritos* 1. Biblioteca Nueva.

Latour, B. (2008). *Reensamblar lo social: Una introducción a la teoría del actor-red*. Ediciones Manantial.

López, M., Tapia-Frade, A., & Ruíz, C. M. (2023). Patologías y dependencias que provocan las redes sociales en los jóvenes nativos digitales. *Revista de Comunicación y Salud: RCyS*, 13(1), 23–43.

Lozano-Muñoz, N., Borrallo-Riego, Á., & Guerra-Martín, M. D. (2022). Influencia de las redes sociales sobre la anorexia y la bulimia en las adolescentes: Una revisión sistemática. *Anales del Sistema Sanitario de Navarra*, 45(2). https://doi.org/10.23938/ASSN.1009.

Martos, E., & Martos, A. (2014). Artefactos culturales y alfabetización en la era digital: Discusiones conceptuales y praxis educativa. *Teoría Educativa*, 26(1), 119–135. DOI: doi:10.14201/teoredu2014261119135.

O'Reilly, K. (2008). *Key concepts in ethnography*. Sage.

Peirce, C. (2012). Abduction and induction. In J. Buchler (Ed.), *Philosophical writings of Peirce* (pp. 150–156). Dover.

Pemberton, S. A. (2016). *Harmful societies: Understanding social harm* (Kindle ed.). Policy Press.

Pérez, J. R. (2017). *We are cyborgs*. Grupo Editorial Criminología y Justicia.

Pink, S., Horst, H., Postill, J., Hjorth, L., Lewis, T., & Tacchi, J. (2016). *Digital ethnography: Principles and practice*. Sage.

Portillo, V., Ávila, J. A., & Capps, J. W. (2021). Relación del uso de redes sociales con la autoestima y la ansiedad en estudiantes universitarios. *Enseñanza en Investigación y Psicología*, 3(1), 139–149.

Raymen, T. (2019). The enigma of social harm and the barrier of liberalism: Why zemiology needs a theory of the good. *Justice, Power and Resistance*, 3(1), 134–163.

Riba, C. (2013). *Métodos cualitativos de investigación en criminología*. FUOC.

Silva, A. (2019). Etnografía [des]encubierta. Una mirada a la práctica etnográfica encubierta del Ultra Realismo criminológico [unpublished master's thesis]. UNED.

Silva, A. (2020). Propuesta denegada. Dilemas éticos en la etnografía encubierta criminológica. *International E-Journal of Criminal Sciences*, 15, art.2.

Silva, A. (2024). Dando forma a las sombras. Comprendiendo la construcción del conocimiento y el dispositivo encubierto en las etnografías del Ultra-Realismo [doctoral dissertation, UNED]. http://e-spacio.uned.es/fez/view/tesisuned:ED-Pg-DivSubSoc-Asilva

Silva, A., Muñoz, M., & Cordero, R. (2023). Ultra-realismo, daño social y su aplicación a entornos de menores. Un análisis de la victimización de menores en RRSS. In J. Rámila, C. Benedicto, & M. Abanades (Eds.), *Jóvenes y menores delincuentes. Problemáticas actuales, perspectivas futuras* (pp. 183–208). Bosch.

Turner, S. (1984). *La explicación sociológica como traducción*. Fondo de Cultura Económica.

Tribunal Constitucional. (2021). *STC 148/2021*, de 14 julio 2021. Disposición 13032 del BOE núm. 182 de 2021.

Vega, J. (2005). Mentes híbridas: Cognición, representaciones externas y artefactos epistémicos. *AIBR, Revista de Antropología Iberoamericana*, noviembre–diciembre.

Velasco, H., & Díaz de Rada, Á. (2013). *La lógica de la investigación etnográfica: Un modelo de trabajo para etnógrafos de la escuela*. Trotta.

Yar, M. (2012). Critical criminology, critical theory and social harm. In S. Hall & S. Winlow (Eds.), *New directions in criminological theory* (pp. 52–65). Routledge.

5 Livestreaming
Building criminological digital storytelling

Much of what we do in the social media is telling stories, the great saga of everyday life in which we (or perhaps our pets, relatives, or friends) play the leading role. Instagram even contains a mosaic (feed) in which you can display carefully selected moments, combining filters, images, and captions: from a vegan pie in Madrid to urban art in Birmingham. Besides this, Instagram has a temporary content function called "stories." There, you can post a survey about your haircut, add techno music while complaining about correcting exams, or post a happy avatar while enjoying some nice organic wine. In this narrative endeavour, the only thing that is often unclear is the genre of our own story: Who am I? A bon vivant with wanderlust, a committed fighter for social justice, or a punk mime? Perhaps all of them at once. As mentioned, there is a wide range of tools available for telling these stories: filters, music, surveys, avatars, emojis, stickers. According to Instagram (2023), "Stories are a quick, easy way to share moments and experiences. Use text, music, stickers and GIFs to bring your story to life," while TikTok's (2023) mission is "to inspire creativity and bring joy."

5.1. Digital storytelling, visual ethnography, and sensory ethnography

In this chapter, we will examine the Storyans[1] workshops conducted with our participants in private accounts on Instagram and TikTok. We will also analyse the work done in the Telegram groups for the A.I.DRIANA project. Throughout this chapter, we will discuss

DOI: 10.4324/9781003399315-5

1 how to keep the young people taking part in the research motivated, and
2 how to engage them in the creation of stories.

Let us recall that the project was part of a sophisticated "digital ethnography" (Pink et al., 2016). However, the storytelling element came as a result of combining several ethnographic strategies: digital ethnography in addition to "sensory ethnography" (Pink, 2015) and "visual ethnography" (Pink, 2021), all with an awareness of "live methods" (Back & Puwar, 2012).

These strategies consistently sought to

a emphasise the fun component of the workshops, creating and playing;
b do research from a horizontal perspective – avoiding academicism but without hiding behind a "disguise"; and
c understand the children's reality on the internet just as it is.

Let us first define visual ethnography. Pink (2021) deems it to be

> a dynamic, reflexive and situated field of practice, which involves researchers engaging with visual and digital methods and media in seeking to collaboratively create and share new ways of knowing and knowledge relating to specific research questions and agendas.
>
> (p. 39)

As defined by this author, visual ethnography becomes an extremely relevant phenomenon in relation to the social media in which to conduct research but also to spread knowledge about that research or about the social reality (p. 43). Furthermore, according to Pink (2021), "when we do visual ethnography, especially when it involves making images with, in ways parallel to and/or for participants, we can become implicated in their visual and digital practices" (p. 56), and therefore these are profoundly reflexive and collaborative practices.

We shall now focus on sensory ethnography. When discussing this strategy, Pink (2015) explains that although it could be said that the senses have always been present in ethnography (seeing, listening, and smelling in the field), it becomes "all the more necessary to re-think ethnography to explicitly account for the senses" (p. 7). Pink (2015) also notes that sensory ethnography is a constantly evolving field (p. 6) and some of its instruments are already associated with ethnography, such as participant observation and interviews. However,

> other less conventional methods may entail more intentional interventions on the part of the researcher. For instance, these could include collaborations such as producing a film, writing a song or inventing a new recipe with one's research participant.
>
> (p. 6)

In sensory ethnography, elicitation is a widely used methodology (Pink, 2015, pp. 87–93) that can prompt participants to reflect on the meaning of images, smells, or sounds, asking the subjects to produce them or attempt to spark emotional reactions in people.

Live methods (Back & Puwar, 2012), in turn, advocate the following as a kind of manifesto (pp. 7–15):

- Developing tools for collaborative and simultaneous real-time research.
- Avoiding the trap of the absolute present, especially in digital research (strongly focused on innovation), and attempting to theorise, imagine, and develop the future.
- Attempting to see the whole picture.
- Doing more crafted, artistic, sociological work, developing new research tools and technologies aimed at fleeing from digital capitalism. The use of multimedia elements, performance, and aesthetic practices is also taken into consideration; also fostering innovation and experimentation.
- Paying attention to the senses when thinking about social issues.
- Fostering the imagination and sociological writing, the liveliness of words and stories.
- Being patient when doing research, avoiding the hectic pace of regulatory agencies and production needs.
- Fleeing from arrogance and salvific paternalism, doing ethical, applicable research that has a positive social impact.

As we can see, digital, visual, and sensory ethnographies have numerous theoretical and methodological elements in common. Visual ethnographies may themselves be conducted in and on social media. Perhaps the easiest way to distinguish them is as follows:

- Sensory ethnography: Focusing on the senses and perception, as well as on the value and meaning these have for the participants. Imagine the feeling of danger or anxiety in response to a violent act (Silva et al., 2020), the drowsiness caused by addiction to the social media, the use of relaxing music to study, the feelings prompted by alcohol, or the study done by Pink (2015) on perceptions of clean and dirty (pp. 85–87).
- Visual ethnography: Focusing on the image, whether videos, photographs, posters, and so forth. Not only studying them but also producing them. One example by Pink (2021) are the research projects done with photographs of female bullfighters in Spain and views on traditional women (pp. 160–162).
- Digital ethnography: Focusing broadly on the use and meaning of technology in people's lives, the study of experiences and practices related to digital environments, and the creation and study of digital contents.

Regarding storytelling, from the perspective of dynamic psychotherapy for children, Brandell (2017) indicates that reciprocal stories require children to create characters, a narrative structure (introduction, climax, etc.), and a conclusion, which may entail a moral lesson (p. 5). He also makes reference to the key points of the children's stories (pp. 12–13): a) the dynamic theme; b) the object relations scenario and self- and object representations; c) the affective tone of the story; d) paralinguistic, visual, and kinesic cues; and e) the child's defensive behaviours, discrete defences, defensive strategies, and conflict-free solutions. That is, what Brandell (2017, pp. 12–13) suggests is that in all children's stories, the therapist must identify what the story is about, the conflict being addressed, how the child portrays him-/herself and in relation to parents, relatives, and so forth, the emotions expressed (boredom, anticipation, fear, etc.), how these emotions change, what kind of body language the child uses when telling them, and whether this varies greatly from the tone of the story. Finally, consideration must be given to the solutions to the conflicts raised. In our workshops, the approach was related to research rather than therapeutic, but certain issues can be taken into consideration, always bearing in mind the unique features of narrations on Instagram and TikTok:

a   The limited duration of videos on the applications and the desire for immediacy
b   The static nature of photographs
c   The combination of symbols: images, captions, and so forth
d   The interactive nature of some narrations: questions, invitations, and so forth

Based on the above, the reader may be wondering, How did we define "storytelling" in our projects? The answer would be that it is defined as creating and using characters in private social media platforms to narrate projective fantasy stories that are either self-contained (lasting one video, one post, etc.) or represent a continuity across one or more of these social networks. Holding simultaneous workshops to discuss and prepare the stories.

5.2. The Storyans workshop

Specifically, in our project, each of our participants (Storyans) had to post a total of ten entries[2] (five on each social platform) during the course of the workshops and meet weekly to discuss them. In these entries, they could use filters, disguises, surveys, stickers, emojis, and so forth. They could take advantage of all the functions on the social media platforms used but always had to portray one of the characters created, with their specific traits, tone, attire, and so on. The Storyans had to depict scenes from the youths' daily lives related to the use of the internet and social media. They were asked to have the stories happen to the characters but did not necessarily have to be their own personal experiences. That is, depending on the character type, these could be their own, vicarious, or intuitively imagined experiences.[3]

A total of 14 meetings were planned for the workshops. The meeting schedules were sent by email each week, with daily reminders in the Telegram group. The occupational diversity of the sample (featuring parent management) forced us to hold around three meetings per week, which would have an impact on the project development. A group was set up on Telegram, given that this was deemed the most secure platform in light of the ethical reflections stemming from the MARVEL protocol (Silva, 2024). It must be emphasised that the motivation behind all our actions throughout the research was always the safety and well-being of the children.

5.2.1. Creating the characters: Satire, diversity, and aspiration

The first three meetings were used to create the different characters (Annex 3), broken down into subgroups for this task instead of doing this all together, as was expected. This made it more difficult for the sample to understand some of the characters, prompting an excessive use of some characters to the detriment of others. Although it is true that the initial process of creating the characters was fruitful and enriching, as a general rule content creation was more laborious. To encourage a more entertaining atmosphere, character sheets were used as part of the "Player's Manual" in a simple process taken from role-playing games. The sheets to be filled out had to specify the age, gender, character's appearance (including whether filters, glasses, wigs, and so forth were used), and their tastes and interests.

Certain elements were observed when the characters were created:

a   A spontaneous enthusiasm for diversity in gender and sexual orientation: When asked about the defining features of the characters, the Storyans chose, of their own will, a wide range of sexual orientations and gender identities. They came up with characters that were asexual (A.I.Driana), pansexual (Newton-20), heterosexual (D.J. Green), and also non-binary (Spirit). The concept of "new masculinities" was mentioned when D.J. Green was designed, and the "hetero-basic" concept was added to the glossary.

b   The creation of outsiders and a taste for satire: A.I.Driana was created not as an aspirational avatar but as a satirical game to ridicule "posh" attitudes, overconsumption, and so forth. The Storyans themselves admitted that they knew many people like that. However, that satire later faded away and the A.I.Driana character was used extensively out of convenience. Other characters, like Newton-20, are out of place: "200 years [old] they created it in 1822 and it was disconnected until being reactivated in 2022. Knows nothing about the world" (character sheet), Spirit "is an alien from Pluto, sent to Earth because they didn't want him (he was the black sheep with different powers and they were embarrassed), he was adopted by a millionaire in New York City" (character sheet), and D.J. Green "when he goes to university he paints himself white [he is green], puts on a hat or hood and acts 'hetero-basic' to avoid bullying" (character sheet).

c   The mishmash: Many of the characters are a mixture of concepts taken from comics, cartoons, and pop culture. For example, Spirit (whose favourite shape to transform into is a horse) is inspired by an animated film of the same name and also draws from the trope of the superhero from another planet that is adopted by a millionaire. Newton-20 is a 19th-century robot with cyberpathic and telepathic powers and more. Perhaps the character in which this is seen most sharply is Bundy González, who experienced a hastier creative process: he is a basketball and football player from a rich family but also a criminal investigator accompanied by a ghost. Finally, he was assigned the stereotype of being the "very funny Andalusian" (character sheets).

d   Mythomania and wealth: These are cross-cutting themes across several characters. A.I.Driana is obsessed with shopping and handbags and in love with herself, D.J. Green is a famous makeup influencer who speaks arrogantly and changes hairstyles, Spirit is adopted by a millionaire from New York, and Bundy González comes from a wealthy family.

In conclusion, it could be said that certain projections and aspirations related to adolescence (difference, search for identity, etc.) were observed in the character creation process that were later not explored thoroughly in the creation of content. A taste for satire with certain elements that give a sense of something undesirable also emerges, as well as the influence of popular culture.

Annex 3 shows that the characters used most often across the different social media platforms were A.I.Driana and Newton-20. However, the limited use of the Instagram feed ($n = 2$), compared to Instagram stories ($n = 17$) is worth noting. This could be understood from three perspectives: a) the cultural impact that the stories function, which is more dynamic and interactive, has among young people, b) a stronger desire for that which is fleeting among young people, and c) a greater desire to be less exposed.

In relation to these issues, we observed that most of the stories content was posted using "mischief" (Table 5.1), meaning that the participants chose to post content in which they did not appear (even though they were playing their characters through captions and images) or they are shown from the back or in disguise. It should be noted that there were no express instructions in the "Player's Manual" indicating that posting this kind of content was not allowed.

5.2.2. *Informal meetings and group dynamics*

Regarding the scheduled meetings, it should be pointed out that it was impossible to hold any meetings in which all the participants were present. Because of the academic activities they were involved in and their parents' time management, it was necessary to hold two or three meetings per week. Sometimes there was just one person in attendance. For this reason, it is crucial to plan research well in advance, also bearing in mind the children's exam periods, holidays, and extracurricular activities.

All of this had a profound impact on the group dynamics, the creation and understanding of the characters, and the motivation to post material. Another matter to bear in mind is the use of the

Table 5.1 Use of mischief

Content posted with mischief	Instagram feed	Instagram stories	TikTok	Character total
A.I.Driana	0	4	1	5
Newton-20	0	1	0	1
Spirit	0	0	0	0
D.J. Green	0	2	0	2
Bundy González	0	2	1	3
Platform total	0	9	2	

Source: Compiled by authors. Madrid, 2023.

Telegram chat group for communication with the participants. A safe, friendly environment was sought to convey the spirit of the meetings, but it ended up being ineffective due to the lack of familiarity with the application. The Telegram group was operative, but it ultimately was used as a system for announcing the meetings and providing links to them. Often, the participants reported that they were not available.

> Yea, I'll post things this week, I've been busy.
>
> (Telegram message, 3 May 2022, 21:49)

> Today is really bad for me.
>
> (Telegram message, 21 April 2022, 14:26)

One young woman was identified as having no interest in the project but was taking part at her parents' behest. This sparks a fundamental reflection that must be addressed from an ethical perspective:[4] *Do the children want to be here? Do they feel comfortable? Are they having fun?* In other cases, the connections needed to assign tasks or produce knowledge as a group were just not there.

> Okay, everyone, today at the meeting we raised the idea of doing a video by several of you, doing an interview of Newton-20, tentatively there should be several characters, and it will be posted this week. There is no problem in doing it with more people. Anyone up for it?
>
> (Telegram message, 19 April 2022, 19:06)

This idea of creating a video among several Storyans using the Newton-20 character, for example, was never carried out despite numerous reminders and surveys. Issues of engagement and continuity were among the most significant limitations of the project, given that in relation to Telegram,[5] they admitted that they were not very familiar with the tool and would have preferred to use WhatsApp. Furthermore (and closely linked to the above), the fact that they had to download the platform just for the project meant that they did not check it regularly.

Therefore, the focus of the meetings was shifted toward a hybrid approach between storytelling and an informal focus group (in which all manner of topics related to the content created and the internet experience was discussed). This proved to be more productive, generating enriching reflections on the social media, their impact on the youngsters' lives, or the workshop's creative process.

5.2.3. *Important information about the creative process*

It must be pointed out that one of the most relevant factors revealed about the creative process is related to content perfection. The participants felt that the content posted on the internet had to be exquisite because it exposed the young people to an audience.[6] On several occasions, the Storyans were asked during the workshops why they had not yet posted any content or what content they planned to post, reminding them of the commitment they had made:

> Saray is waiting for materials [which she ordered to make a video] to arrive because she does not want to make just any [video].
>
> (Field journal excerpt, Jorge R. Pérez)

The participants were often somewhat embarrassed due to the failure to create a sense of belonging and community. As Roy mentioned, both he and Lara would have preferred everyone to be together and share ideas so they could all contribute. After some time, Yaira also explained that she felt less embarrassed, but she also admitted that TikTok was going to be hard.

It is worth contemplating from an educational viewpoint whether that pressure jeopardises the children's capacity to express themselves by pushing them to create well-prepared content with an appearance of "false" spontaneity. Participants at several meetings also admitted that the character they used the most was A.I.Driana because it was the easiest to portray, and in addition, they saw in her people they knew. Given that this character was conceived as a type of parody, one might also ask the following:

a   Whether the character is grotesque: Gus remarked that A.I. Driana wants to make people jealous, using numerous handbags and prices, because he believes people behave like this in real life, especially famous people. He then mentioned the "posh" music used in the video.

b   Whether the character is aspirational in terms of a luxury lifestyle, holidays, handbags, shopping, and so forth: One of the participants admitted they "have things in common," which is why this was her favourite character.

c   Whether the character is a generational symbol, representing the status quo of digital culture.

d   Whether the character has (or needs) a feminist reading, especially when it is used by the boys, perhaps as an expression of a distorted idea of femininity.

5.3. Lessons learned

Now that we have discussed these matters related to the creative process, let us return to the questions raised at the beginning of the chapter about how to spark emotions and feelings in young people and engage them in the stories. To do this, we must refresh our memories, indicating once again that the workshops were based on sensory (Pink, 2015) and visual (Pink, 2021) ethnographies with a pervading live method philosophy (Back & Puwar, 2012). As noted above, we view ethnography as a research logic rather than a closed methodological technique. From this perspective, the reader is encouraged to bear in mind three key elements in planning research involving children: reflexivity, creativity, and playfulness.

5.3.1. Reflexivity

In this case, we are referring to the researcher's role and position in the research but also to the collective creation of knowledge mentioned above (Pink, 2021), particularly in the audiovisual realm. Whereas all the entries posted on TikTok and Instagram were designed and made by the participants (as well as the character design), knowledge was created collectively during the weekly workshops and in the Telegram group.

The weekly workshops, which were aimed at aiding the participants in the creative process and fostering this process, in addition to answering any questions they had in this regard, ended up as authentic informal online focus groups (Clark et al., 2021, pp. 467–472) where topics were discussed without restrictions. The workshop structure entailed introducing oneself and chatting about the week, discussing the content that the Storyans had posted, asking whether they had had experiences similar to the ones depicted in the content discussed, asking about the chosen characters, the difficulties encountered and how they felt during the process, as well as filling out the "Player's Manual" glossary. Over the course of the meetings, they reflected as a group on topics such as safety in the social media, the pressures of social media, each person's hobbies, relationships with parents, and so forth. They also solved problems related to the use of the platforms. Sometimes, in a "live method" exercise (Back & Puwar, 2012), the content posted during the week was viewed and discussed with the workshop participants since some of them had not had a chance to see it beforehand.

> We look at the entries together. While viewing it, they remark on it with a pleasant smile. . . . Gus liked the content and feels it is original. It conveyed the posh character's profile and he found it believable. Yaira is embarrassed and thought it was funny; it helped her with how to talk.
>
> (Field journal excerpt, Jorge R. Pérez)

In addition, they shared ideas about future content, although many times it was not actually created due to the participants' difficulties[7] in creating content on certain characters or due to concerns about making the content perfect and, particularly, due to the difficulty in creating videos together. Some of the ideas discussed at the workshops that never came to fruition were

- A.I.Driana, on holiday, meets people who recognise her because she is somewhat famous and they ask to take pictures of her;
- Newton-20 is interviewed in the media;
- Spirit (who has the power to communicate with animals) talking to their dog; and
- Bundy González discussing the score of a Lakers game that the ghost who helps him solve cases confided to him.

In turn, the Telegram group, as mentioned before, was used to announce the meetings[8] but also to try to help the Storyans create content. In some cases, surveys were used to persuade them to create joint videos but without success.

5.3.2. Creativity

Throughout the entire project, stimulating the participants' creativity became an essential element. They were always encouraged to create content however they wanted, to record videos together, to create their own material to record,[9] to experiment with filters and music, to feel completely free when creating their stories. It is worth noting the humorous and satirical content of many videos like the Vlogs on A.I.Driana's holidays, attempting to ridicule the character's excessive hedonism:

> HIIIII TODAY I SPENT THE ENTIRE DAY AT A SHOP-PING CENTRE IN MARBELLA, BOUGHT MYSELF TWO MEGACHEAP HANDBAGS (450 € EACH) AND NOW IT'S TIME TO RELAX AND WATCH A SERIES WHICH I'LL TELL YOU LATER IF I LIKE IT SO I MEAAAN GREAT FUN @MARBELLABEACHHOTEL @NETFLIXES
>
> (A.I.Driana Instagram story)

On another occasion, a Storyan posted a physical comedy video of Spirit in which the character trips over a chair and lets out a profanity, which is censored by an angry emoji over its face.

Another expression of creativity mentioned above was the use of what we have referred to as mischief (Table 5.1). Some illustrative examples of expressions of this technique used to enhance the stories were

- taking photos of green beverage bottles with captions aimed at engaging the viewer, which also prevented the character from being shown;
- recording images of fans arriving at a football match to simulate that Bundy González was part of the audience; and
- using photographs of handbags or pristine beaches to portray A.I.Driana's purchases and holidays.

5.3.3. Playfulness

It is very important for the participants to have fun and enjoy activities of this kind, as creativity emerges when they feel comfortable and relaxed. In addition, it is very hard to hold that interest throughout the research project. In our research, we decided to concentrate the entire storytelling phase into one month (not including the Easter holidays) to harness that immediacy and endeavour to keep them engaged.

Instead of sending "orthodox" instructions about the research, the entertainment proposal was emphasised through the use of the "Player's Manual." Furthermore, the players were referred to as Storyans. The Storyans were also encouraged to use all the possible functions on TikTok and Instagram (music, tags, surveys, open questions). Throughout the discussions held in the workshops and in many of the Telegram messages, the participants were asked to have fun, and the use of an informal, relaxed, non-scholarly tone was crucial when holding the meetings, discussing comics, science fiction, reading, films, and series. One of the main problems when it comes to creating an entertainment proposal is that the participants have diverse maturity levels,[10] but by holding the workshops in smaller groups (although this was not the original intention), it was easier to create different groups with similar interests. Furthermore, close attention was consistently paid to the following:

a   The Storyans' interests and hobbies, sharing some of them with the researchers. This helped generate rapport.
b   The sensitivity of each person when discussing delicate or more taboo topics, encouraging them to take part in the discussion but not forcing opinions or judging.

As we near the end of this chapter, we are certain that the reader has numerous ideas (as well as eagerness and logical concern) as to how to conduct research with young people that entails elicitation, storytelling, sensory elements, playfulness, and digital environments. Some examples, merely for illustrative purposes, might be as follows:

•   Poster presentations: Where the boys and girls make posters or brochures on diverse situations using tools such as Canva. These posters could then be displayed or posted online, asking the children to create a short audiovisual report (using Instagram reels, for example) about the presentation and to reflect on it. A full red-carpet event.

- Video game script: Engaging the children in the creation of a simple video game on the topic being studied, designing characters, storylines, and challenges that could later be produced by university students, volunteers, and others, and handed out to children and adolescents.
- A cross-media graphic encyclopaedia: Where boys and girls create graphics (on concepts such as cybercrime or IT security, for example) that are later posted on public Twitter (now X) and Instagram accounts, encouraging people to add comments or reflect on them.

In relation to the above, it should be noted that the GCIPS *Guía de buenas prácticas sobre el uso de redes sociales* (Best practices guide on the use of social media) (Pérez et al., 2023) published by UNAF[11] contains activities, classroom games, and similar reflections. This guide is a free resource stemming from the projects discussed here, which aims to transfer knowledge symmetrically: with clear and simple non-academic language, geared towards (using different registers) families, educators, and young people. In sum, research with young people must generate a positive impact on society, building bridges and forging networks of support and dialogue.

Notes

1 The name is a play on words in Spanish and English, and it was introduced to the participants in this way in the "Player's Manual."
2 On Instagram, they could upload content onto the feed (central tiles) and to stories (temporary content). To keep the stories from being lost, a highlights collection was created for each character.
3 Most of the characters were older than our Storyans; some of them were already university students and others were legendary beings.
4 The fact that they are forced to participate by their parents not only prompts a social desirability bias or lack of engagement but also leads them to be classified as non-agents. Taking an in-depth look at the relationships between parents and children was crucial to our project.
5 Telegram was used for ethical reasons because it is more secure.
6 We might recall that all the platforms used in this project were totally private.
7 Many of these difficulties arose from having created characters with numerous details – colours, accents, fantasy characters, and so forth – that they were later unable to portray, as in the case of Spirit.
8 Stickers and GIFs were used in the messages as a more familiar code.

9 Remember that D.J. Green was a green character and Newton-20 would always be portrayed in black and white. In turn, the Spirit character had a very unique pendant and the Storyans were encouraged to cut it out, draw it, and so forth at the character creation meetings.

10 In our case, some of the older participants were more interested in going out, playing sports, and so on, while others were more focused on political and social issues, an interest in video games, or reading.

11 Union of Family Associations/Unión de Asociaciones Familiares – UNAF, in conjunction with the Spanish Ministry for Social Affairs and the 2030 agenda.

References

Back, L., & Puwar, N. (2012). A manifesto for live methods: Provocations and capacities. *The Sociological Review*, 60(S1), 6–17. https://doi.org/10.1111/j.1467-954X.2012.02114.x.

Brandell, J. R. (2017). *Of mice and metaphors: Therapeutic storytelling with children*. Sage.

Clark, T., Foster, L., Sloan, L., & Bryman, A. (2021). *Bryman's social research methods* (6th ed.). Oxford University Press.

Instagram. (2023). *Instagram stories*. about.instagram.com.

Pérez, J. R., Díaz, J., Muñoz, M., Cordero, R., & Silva, A. (2023). *Guía de buenas prácticas sobre el uso de redes sociales*. UNAF.

Pink, S. (2015). *Doing sensory ethnography* (2nd ed.). Sage.

Pink. S. (2021). *Doing visual ethnography*. Sage.

Pink, S., Horst, H., Postill, J., Hjorth, L., Lewis, T., & Tacchi, J. (2016). *Digital ethnography: Principles and practice*. Sage.

Silva, A. (2024). Dando forma a las sombras. Comprendiendo la construcción del conocimiento y el dispositivo encubierto en las etnografías del Ultra-Realismo [doctoral dissertation, UNED]. http://e-spacio.uned.es/fez/view/tesisuned:ED-Pg-DivSubSoc-Asilva

Silva, A., Muñoz, J., & Margalef, A. (2020). Gender experience: Metodología experimental para el estudio de la ciudad y la inseguridad desde una perspectiva feminista. *Antropología Experimental*, 20, 199–209. https://doi.org/10.17561/rae.v20.14b.

TikTok. (2023). *About TikTok*. http://www.tiktok.com/about.

6   Just chatting

A gathering of future challenges

The proposed methodologies we have described in this book will likely have sparked a number of questions. Most of these doubts are probably related to how to align the new kind of society in which we are living today and the world of research. The new era that has been unfolding for more than a decade now, along with the emergence of new technologies and AI, demand and call for new ways of living in the world. This cultural shift has affected every facet of social life: from the most intimate and personal to the collective level, from the very young to the very old, from entertainment to work life, from practice to theory. Obviously, ethnography has not been immune to this upheaval, the aftershocks of which are expected to continue.

6.1. Science and its idols

Ever since what we know today as science emerged in Greece, not a single historical mutation has arisen that was not accompanied by a question about the scientific method, the *méthodos*. The modern era, for example, would never have seen the light without questioning those issues of the right "way," the appropriate *hodos* to take to uncover the secrets of nature. To do this, many scientific practices rendered stagnant by ancient scholasticism had to be left behind. *Discourse on the Method* (2011)[1], which Descartes served as an appetiser to his mathematics, or Francis Bacon's *Novum organum scientiarum* (1984) are two of the most extraordinary examples of that historic moment. The historians of the future will be the ones to place labels on what is happening to us today, perhaps choosing some of the terms

DOI: 10.4324/9781003399315-6

proposed in recent times – postmodernity, cybermodernity, selficity – but it is in our hands to develop the best methodology to suitably guide what we do, our way of doing research.

In addition and prior to analysing the properties of the object of study, all methodological work must entail a weeding of practices of the past (and the present) that hinder the research. Descartes, for example, had to demolish the entire previous scientific edifice, including the foundations, and start over from scratch. Even more astutely, Bacon identified the vices that hindered research work, calling them *idola*, for they were worshipped as idols. According to Bacon, these idols could be found in human nature itself (*idola tribu*), in education (*idola speculus*), in language (*idola fori*), and even in philosophy (*idola theatri*). Each period in history produces its own mythology with the idols that uphold it, and our era is no different, either on a scientific or social level. As the reader will have realised, we too have had to identify and overcome the idolatry of our time.[2]

One of the first idols we have endeavoured to isolate is structural, which means it is very difficult to break free from its omnipresent coordinates. Perhaps it could be called the "commercial idol." As the reader will recall, we addressed this idol in Chapter 2 in reference to its ties to the academic world. The new era now underway coincides with a determination to commercialise broad sectors of society, erasing or confounding any community public space. This involves not only declaring that everything is marketable but also exporting the business management model to every field of human relationability. Several decades ago, it was already noted that this proliferation "of the 'enterprise' form within the social body is what is at stake in neo-liberal policy" (Foucault, 2004, p. 154). The educational setting managed to resist the onslaught of the market for quite a while. The field of research also remained largely unscathed, due largely to the democratisation of knowledge discussed in Chapter 2. But short-term profitability and market interests are now what determine not only *which* topics must be studied and what is worth spending money on but also *how* that knowledge must be produced, subject to standards of efficiency imported from the market (Rhoades & Slaughter, 2010, p. 45).

It is an utter tragedy that the ultimate decision about what is researched comes from offices and dynamics unrelated to university dynamics, for this makes it increasingly difficult to earmark funds for basic research, for example, on which the future of our society rests, even for the development of technology. By definition, the market will always be blind to those future possibilities of basic research. It would be naive at this point to believe that we could return to a completely public model because even top-level governmental decisions are affected by private interests. However, it would be necessary to once again implement democratic channels at all levels of education and in academia. We feel that social science research like the kind we have done in the projects presented here is crucial and essential to making our world a better place, particularly, as in our case, when it is about young people, the living matter on which the future is built.

6.2. The great universe of young people: Ethics and fluidity

How should we deal with these age groups? They are defined by a great degree of variability, and working ethically is essential here. Working with young people in a diverse age range (12–15 years old) made us realise that we could not treat all of these age groups in the same way. Despite the nearness in age, they have very diverse circumstances and could even feel humiliated if they are classified in an age group other than their own. In addition, as mentioned in Chapter 3, rigid moral protocols encumber research on a reality marked by unpredictability. Our approach and proposal was to implement situated ethics, constructed within the context of the research as it is done. Shying from all-encompassing stances, ethics in this regard must also be dialogic. Thus, we feel that a consensus must be reached with the field agents, avoiding preset moral criteria. In response to these issues and in an effort to avoid what might be called the "deductive idol," we used the MARVEL protocol (Silva, 2024; see Annex 2).

What is youth like today? These new times are characterised by a decline in closed, essentialist identities. The new cyberworld has made it easier to release ways of being that used to be repressed. Early on in this cyber era, authors like Wajcman (2006) noted that "virtual reality is a new space for undermining old social relations, a place of freedom and liberation from conventional gender roles" (p. 12). Furthermore, the issue of feminism in this area helps depatriarchalize technology, which served to biologize and naturalize women in the past. Therefore, we are confronted with the fourth wave, that of cyberfeminism or feminism 4.0. Of course, this denaturalization also entails the possibility of inventing new ontologies of what is human, even post-human ones, somewhere between "the technical, organic, mythic, textual, and political" (Haraway, 1999, p. 154). In our work with young people, we confirmed that openness to being human (Agamben, 2010) in which options that were once forbidden or unknown are given an opportunity.

Thus, in the workshops, we saw that the digital world offered a chance to construct different characters that break away from any naturalist-binary stance and the prevailing normativity of the analogue world. In the storytelling workshops, as described in Chapter 5, the children deconstructed that binarism, choosing a wide range of sexual orientations and cyberqueer gender identities. If the digital ethnography proposal is flexible, hybrid, open to dialogue, and cross-disciplinary, the reason is that the reality we are dealing with has those same characteristics and aspirations. Ethnography must adapt and situate itself, following Machado's recommendation about making the way (*méthodos*) as we walk because reality is ever changing "always in becoming, always incomplete" (Deleuze, 1997, p. 15). As we have suggested before, closed protocols are a shot in the foot to the ethnographer and an affront to reality.

How should we watch, observe young people? Given the variability and mutability we have described above, it is important not to allow our hands to be tied by any preset formulas. Depending on the circumstances, the complete observer approach, for example, could be taken, as we have done in CONFIDOMINA2. Likewise, participant stances, while they affect the outcome of what is observed, are also necessary in our research. However, we have pointed out that bearing in mind all ethical considerations, covert practices are much more common in everyday life than is generally presumed (Simmel, 2019), and they should not be identified with malpractice. Currently, speaking in terms of dualities like open or covert instead of considering intensities or degrees (Kockelman, 2016) is incoherent. This is especially true because, depending on the context, the use of a covert device or artifact could be more effective in not disturbing the dynamics in the field or its agents (Silva, 2024).

6.3.   Promises and problems of digital citizenship

Although it is true that the digital space is loaded with promises, it also hosts numerous dangers and challenges. What started out years ago as a democratic agora is quickly becoming a completely deregulated cyberbazaar. Influencers or content creators, which have ousted the traditional role models, often provide models of conduct based on excessive luxury and aesthetic dictatorship. Because young people also have their own idols. Even so, in our workshops, we detected a sense of ambivalence toward unchecked hyper-consumerism. We not only found aspirationalism and a feeling of identifying with that world but also irony, like that shown toward the "posh girl" in the Storyans workshops.

Issues of addiction to screens, video games, and short videos at very early ages, a lack of empathy toward real life, and the viral spread of harmful models (fatphobia, LGBTI-phobia, sexism, toxic masculinity, excessive sexualisation at early ages), in addition to what could be classified as crimes prompt that sometimes irreparable "social harm" we spoke of. Our task consists not only in detecting those added problems (and the ethnographies presented here have been of great help to us) but also in proposing solutions[3] that foster a new, more democratic, horizontal digital citizenship, "the idea of virtual consensual community" (Haraway, 1999, p. 151). New tools must be invented to bridge the gap between generations, to foster a more equitable, more feminist, and less patriarchal society. All of this can be done on numerous levels of reality, but it becomes especially relevant in terms of education. Digital citizenship is not just about having democratic access to resources, meaning that we all have access to broadband and 5G. Responsible use is also essential, and this is achieved through knowledge and respect for our rights and those of others. Only in this way can we prevent the risks linked to the use of new technology. And as we have said before, the field of education is fundamental in this regard.

Notes

1 We must not forget, of course, that other Cartesian methodological monument, *Rules for the Direction of the Mind*. Written in 1628, ten years after Bacon's *Novum organum*, the rules represent the most rationalist methodological approach.

2 Although Bacon's identification of idols is one of the cornerstones of any serious methodology, it should be clear by now that throughout this book, we do not identify with his epistemological proposal in which understanding means dominating and judging nature (Hadot, 2004, p. 348). As a man of his time, Bacon was not free from the ideological shadow of its techno-scientific paradigm, which he worshipped with no sense of shame. Perhaps our iconoclastic leanings are more closely aligned with the Nietzschean current, that of *Twilight of the Idols* (2013), full of philosophies of difference and, as such, of the feminist struggles of the 20th and 21st centuries and queer theory.

3 See Annex 4.

References

Agamben, G. (2010). *Lo abierto. El hombre y el animal*. Pre-textos.

Bacon, F. (1984). *Novum organum*. Orbis

Deleuze, G. (1997). *Crítica y clínica*. Anagrama.

Descartes, R. (2011). *Discurso del método*. Alianza.

Descartes, R. (2018). *Reglas para la dirección del espíritu*. Alianza.

Foucault, M. (2004). *Naissance de la biopolitique*. Gallimard.

Hadot, P. (2004). *Le voile d'Isis. Essai sur l'histoire de lidée de nature*. Gallimard.

Haraway, D. (1999). Las promesas de los monstruos. Una política regeneradora para otros inapropiados/bles. *Política y Sociedad*, 30, 121–163.

Kockelman, P. (2016). Grading, gradients, degradation, grace. Part 2: Phenomenology, materiality, and cosmology. *HAU: Journal of Ethnographic Theory*, 6(3), 337–365.

Machado, A. (2020). *Campos de castilla*. Diskolos.

Nietzsche, F. (2013). *El crepúsculo de los ídolos*. Alianza.

Rhoades, G., & Slaughter, S. (2010). Capitalismo académico en la nueva economía. Retos y decisiones. *Pasajes*, 33, 43–59.

Silva, A. (2024). Dando forma a las sombras. Comprendiendo la construcción del conocimiento y el dispositivo encubierto en las etnografías del Ultra-Realismo [doctoral dissertation, UNED]. http://e-spacio.uned.es/fez/view/tesisuned:ED-Pg-DivSubSoc-Asilva

Simmel, G. (2019). *El secreto y las sociedades secretas*. Sequitur.

Wajcman, J. (2006). *El tecnofeminismo*. Cátedra.

Annex 1

Table A.1 Sequential methodological design sheet for CBR

Phases	Phase definition	Response to each phase[1]
Big idea	What concept/idea serves as inspiration for the challenge?	
Essential question	What problem do we have?	
Any others	What challenge do we propose? For whom?	
Guiding questions	What should we respond to?	
Guiding activities	What do we need to do to achieve the final challenge?	
Guiding resources	Where can I find information about how to achieve the challenge?	
Organisation	How should the students be grouped? How is the activity going to be organised if it is cross-disciplinary?	
Solution assessment plan	What assessment tools are we going to use?	
Communication	How are we going to communicate the results?	

Source: Compiled by Cordero et al., 2021, pp. 23–24.

Note: [1]This column should be filled in by the instructor when the proposal about a specific topic of research is made in the classroom.

Annex 2

Name:			
Age:	Gender:	Institution:	
Research objective:	Place:	Period:	

Mark with an X the score that you consider closest to the action taken (1 yes, 4 no)

BEFORE RESEARCH/DESIGN	1 (Yes)	2	3	4 (No)
1. Have I written an ethical framework before starting research?				
2. Is there an ethical committee or similar institution auditing me?				
3. Is informed consent adaptative and gradual?				
4. Are there any contextual/personal background elements that interfere with the research?				
5. Have I negotiated with any gatekeeper the norms accepted by the community?				
Comments				

DURING RESEARCH/FIELDWORK	1 (Yes)	2	3	4 (No)
6. Do those researched understand the field as public?				
7. Is my treatment symmetrical with the people studied?				
8. Did I reward any agent to obtain information?				
9. Is informed consent proving effective?				
10. Are the normative ethical guidelines contrary to those of the field?				
Comments				

AFTER RESEARCH/ANALYSIS AND DISSEMINATION	1 (Yes)	2	3	4 (No)
11. Do I treat/store the data anonymously and confidentially?				
12. Have I written a section on ethics and methodology?				
13. Is my analysis sensationalist?				
14. Would anyone understand the results?				
15. Have I validated my final report with the people in the field?				
Comments				

Figure A.1 MARVEL protocol

Instructions for use

The objective of this document is that the 15 exposed variables are understood in depth. This is essential to guarantee a gradual and flexible reflection on the aspects considered essential in the development of ethnographic research with reference to ethical questions. This protocol has been designed considering the field of social sciences, not a specific area of knowledge. Therefore, it will be useful to establish a dialogue

between it and the ethical code of the discipline of the researcher. In this way, the ethnographer will obtain a reflective and normative perspective. However, this criterion is not mandatory since the functionalities of the two spectra are different despite orbiting in field ethics. The protocol will NOT be carried out once but in each research phase the corresponding block. In the case of having a start and end date for the field stay, complete the "During research" block in the first and second quarter. If there is not a defined date, carry out a review of the issues of said block every month.

1.   Have I considered the ethical framework for the methodological proposal and the objectives of the study? Do I plan to make checks during different research processes to observe the degree of compliance and/or make negotiated and situated adaptations? Have I reflected on issues such as time, money, employment, and conflict of interest? Can the actions that I propose cause harm to the subject by recalling traumatic issues? If yes, did I reflect on potential alternatives? Will my actions tentatively respect the principles of vulnerability, harm, and respect?

2.   If not, have I carried out the aforementioned work? Am I the one who will create a reflective code of ethics during the research? Does anyone else have access to that document to critically examine it?

3.   Have I foreseen that it can be written or oral? Is it presented in terms and language that people in the field can understand? Are the institutions that endorse me known to them? If not, have I asked how to make my credibility strong? Have I honestly developed the objectives and methods of my study? Was it possible? Have I considered that if these are modified, I must also inform the subjects in a way adapted to their particularities? Am I open to modify the consent with the opinions/demands of the study subjects?

4.   Are there any impediments? How will I control possible biases or personal harm? Does the nature of the field force me to deploy covert tactics? Do I base the previous estimation on the past experiences (experiential or related to research)?

5.   Are these norms consistent with the ethical framework? Would it be preferable to adjust the slang, attire, or companionship in the field for better integration with the native? Is the use of a mobile device or field notebook possible during the stay in this area?

6.   Do they understand it as public only for a number of issues and as private for others? Do they believe that the field is fully private? Are we facing public-private spaces? What is the intersubjective framework that governs the field in this regard? Do my field actions obey the conception that the subjects have of the privacy of this one?

7.   What have I done to claim that perspective? Why do I think I got it? Do people in the field consider my position to be symmetrical? Am I acting reciprocally? How am I validating the information? Do I speck the same language/slang as the population?

8.   Have I paid someone in any way (meals, books, influences, information, etc.)? For what reason? Could I have obtained that information in another way? What was stopping me from doing it that "other way"?

9.   Have I been able to use it in writing or orally? If not, for what reasons? Can I solve this in another way? Are the study subjects giving relevance to consent in the model presented to them? Have you understood the objectives of the research and your rights? What guidelines do people in the field value most as informed consent beyond the normative model? Would this be accepted by an ethical committee? Has informed consent been postponed until the later phase of data collection? If yes, what was the reason?

10.   Have I violated any ethical issue? For what reason? Have I changed my ethical approach? Have I done so following the principles of negotiated and situated ethics? Have I consulted with the ethics committee on the issues that are arising in the field? Is the will of the people studied and their rights prevailing? Can I demonstrate this directly? Have I had to deploy covert strategies? Was it because it was the only possible way to obtain information or because there were authorities that did not allow access to it?

11.   Is anonymity guaranteed? That is, it applies to transcripts, places, names, photographs, videos, accents, etc. Is it necessary or has it been an essential condition during the ethnographic process? Is confidentiality limited or absolute? For what reasons? Could anyone use the data against the study population? Do I really have the data safely guarded? Could you improve that security? What will I do with that data when the investigation is done?

12.   Is it a reflective section? Do I present with complete clarity and uncensored the issues that have emerged in the field and the solutions adopted? Do I justify the methodology also based on ethical criteria?

13.   Am I making something up? Am I exaggerating events? For what reasons am I doing any of that? Are they legitimate to people in the field and in order to guarantee their rights? Do they agree? Is it counterproductive for the purpose of the work? Is it related to the objectives of the funding entity? Is it related to economic or personal status issues? Do I carry out an analysis from purely academic categories without using the translation exercise?

14.   Is it in their language? Is the speech appropriate for someone other than academia to understand? Have the data been exposed in a public medium or at the disposal of the sample?

15.   Has it been possible? Have I really tried beyond just one person? Were they willing to do it? Have I modified what they indicated even though it was contrary to my proposal? What reasons could have led me not to try to validate the information?

Annex 3

Table A.2 Creation and usage of characters

Character	A.I.Driana	Newton-20	Spirit	D.J. Green	Bundy González	Total posts per platform
Description	Modern, narcissistic, asexual posh girl in love with herself. Obsessed by consumerism and handbags.	Pansexual, shape-shifting robot in black and white, out of place in today's world. Has telepathic and cyberpathic powers.	Non-binary superhero from another planet capable of converting into animals and communicating with them. Is inclusive and uses a catchphrase in a secret language.	A green heterosexual boy, makeup influencer. Speaks very arrogantly, wears white makeup, and acts differently to avoid being bullied when he is in public.	Funny Andalusian footballer and basketball player who loves sports. He is studying criminal investigation and solves cases with the help of a ghost.	
TikTok	3	3	2	0	2	10
Captions	2	2	2	0	1	7

Character	A.I.Driana	Newton-20	Spirit	D.J. Green	Bundy González	Total posts per platform
Topics	Shopping, holidays, Vlogs	Interview, appearance, search for followers, control over the internet, spying	Humour, shopping	Hobbies	Hobbies	
Instagram feed	1	2	0	0	0	3
Captions	1	2	0	0	0	3
Instagram stories	10	2	0	2	3	17

Source: Compiled by authors. Madrid, 2023.

Annex 4

We offer a series of recommendations below based on our experiences and difficulties. We hope they are helpful in your future research projects.

Caution:

- Mistrust any all-encompassing or deductive rules.
- Ensure the well-being and safety of the children and youths.
- If you come across a taboo subject, do not attempt to pry an opinion from them about the topic. Silence can also be insightful.
- Avoid academic stances in workshops with young people. Remember that horizontality affords good epistemic outcomes.
- Using a relaxed, informal, non-scholarly tone will help achieve that horizontality.
- In relation to this, avoid any kind of paternalism.

Careful with:

- Differences in maturity among the group members may lead to unwanted subgroups.
- The lack of a sense of group or community among young people (who did not know each other previously) can

prompt feelings of embarrassment or shyness in expressing ideas, thus detracting from the research.

- Make sure that all the young participants actually want to be there and that they are under no obligations of any kind. This matter is important to ensure their engagement and continuity.

Pay attention to:

- Plan the activities well in advance, bearing in mind holiday and exam periods; there will be time for fun improvisation later.
- Always use applications that the young people are familiar with and use regularly. Introducing new apps slows down the entire process.
- Try to find common ground and interests to generate a rapport more quickly.
- If an activity does not work as expected, the meeting focus can be shifted and redesigned as you go.

Stimulate:

- Create a sense of fun.
- Foster creativity.
- Encourage humour and "mischief."
- Inspire experimentation and the utmost freedom.

Index

For Product Safety Concerns and Information please contact our EU
representative GPSR@taylorandfrancis.com
Taylor & Francis Verlag GmbH, Kaufingerstraße 24, 80331 München, Germany